JIU JITSU

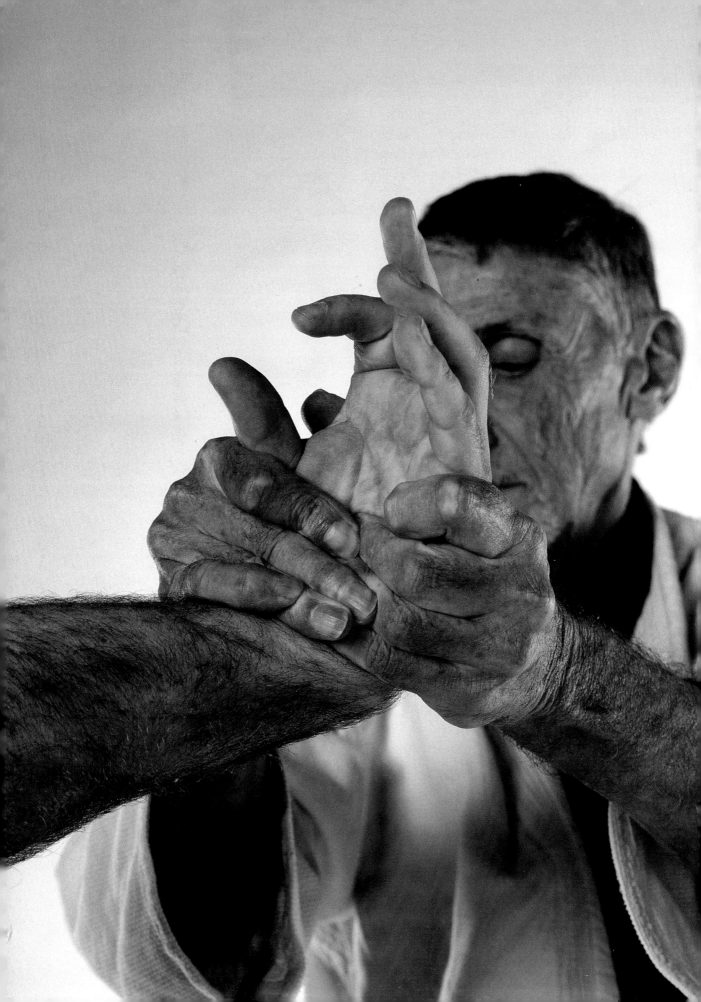

JIU JITSU

Hans-Erik Petermann

NEW
HOLLAND

First published in 2004 by
New Holland Publishers Ltd
London • Cape Town • Sydney • Auckland
www.newhollandpublishers.com

86 Edgware Road
London W2 2EA
United Kingdom

80 McKenzie Street
Cape Town 8001
South Africa

14 Aquatic Drive
Frenchs Forest, NSW 2086
Australia

218 Lake Road
Northcote, Auckland
New Zealand

ISBN 1 84330 595 X (paperback)

PUBLISHER: Mariëlle Renssen
PUBLISHING MANAGERS: Claudia Dos Santos, Simon Pooley
COMMISSIONING EDITOR: Alfred LeMaitre
STUDIO MANAGER: Richard MacArthur
EDITOR: Katja Splettstoesser
DESIGNER: Elmari Kuyler
ILLUSTRATOR: Elmari Kuyler
PICTURE RESEARCHER: Karla Kik
PROOFREADER: Leizel Brown
PRODUCTION: Myrna Collins
CONSULTANT: Allan Tattersall Hanshi (UK Ju-Jitsu Association)
Reproduction by Hirt & Carter (Cape) Pty Ltd
Printed and bound in Malaysia by Times Offset (M) Sdn. Bhd.

2 4 6 8 10 9 7 5 3 1

DISCLAIMER

The author and publishers have made every
effort to ensure that the information con-
tained in this book was accurate at the time
of going to press, and accept no responsibil-
ity for any injury or inconvenience sustained
by any person using this book or following
the advice provided herein.

DEDICATION

For Harry Snowise, my mentor and first jiu jitsu instructor.
Thank you for changing my life and teaching me, by example,
the way of the warrior.

AUTHOR'S ACKNOWLEDGMENTS

I would like to extend my sincere thanks to: all those martial
arts instructors who have taught me so much and with such
patience. My training partners. My students, who have taught
me as much as I have ever taught them and to those who posed
for the photographs. To Nick Aldridge for his wonderful photographic talent and the staff at New Holland Publishers for their
patience with a first-time author.

CONTENTS

INTRODUCTION

Jiu jitsu, which is also known as ju jitsu, is a martial art of Japanese origin that has spread all over the world during the last century and has enjoyed a spectacular renaissance in the last 10 years. This is mostly due to the way in which the Gracie family, who originated and propagated their Brazilian version of the martial art, has taken on and defeated all challengers.

In terms of its technical range, it is one of the most complete martial arts in existence. It includes throws, holds, locks, punches, kicks, strikes, ground grappling, defensive manoeuvres, chokes, resuscitation techniques, defences against weapons as well as, in some jiu jitsu systems, weapons techniques.

The roots of jiu jitsu

Jiu jitsu is usually translated as the 'gentle art' or 'soft technique'. This does not mean that the methods used are harmless or not potentially damaging but rather that you, as the practitioner, do not oppose strength with strength. If someone pushes your chest, for example, you have several options: you can use your strength by bracing yourself against the push or by pushing back. Alternatively, if your timing is good enough through consistent training, you can pivot your body away either just before he makes contact or, as the pressure on your chest increases, thereby removing his target. As he then stumbles past you, you can simultaneously use your foot to trip him and your hand to push him on the back, thus efficiently executing a throwing technique.

This exemplifies the basic principle of the force used in jiu jitsu, which can be compared to bamboo; it will bend and snap back but rarely breaks. The Taoist analogy, which praises the yielding nature of water flowing around a rock, is equally applicable. Whenever you are attacked, strength is exerted and there is, at least momentarily, rigidity. This implies that you can move efficiently around it and counterattack some other suitable target. The nature of human combat is such that every attack opens up one or more weaknesses in the attacker. Jiu jitsu exponents do not meet an attack head-on but attempt to find and utilize these particular weaknesses to their best advantage.

One of the difficulties of getting to grips with the martial art of jiu jitsu is its incredible stylistic diversity. This extends from the medieval battlefield context of throwing techniques, executed in full *samurai* armour, to more than 700 recorded styles in the Tokugawa era; to the birth of Kano's judo; and, finally, to the worldwide

above THE TAOIST ANALOGY OF FLOWING WATER ILLUSTRATES JIU JITSU'S PRINCIPLE OF THE USE OF FORCE.

opposite JIU JITSU IS A CLOSE-RANGE ART EMPHASIZING POTENTIALLY DEADLY TECHNIQUES.

above THE ARMOUR WORN BY *SAMURAI* WARRIORS LIMITED THE UNARMED COMBAT TECHNIQUES THAT COULD BE USED AGAINST THEM.

spread of the art and the current popularity of its Brazilian incarnation. It is challenging to create an easily understandable and coherent overview of such a diverse art.

In ancient and medieval Japan there is no written record of the term 'jiu jitsu'. Before the battle of Sekigahara in 1600 and the subsequent rise of the Tokugawa Shogunate — a time of peace and prosperity that spanned an unbroken succession of 15 *shoguns* until 1868 — Japan had been plagued by ongoing warfare between various powerful *samurai* clans. These warriors knew that their survival on the battlefield depended on the extent and quality of their training. This training, which was extensive, included horsemanship, swimming in armour, the tying up of captives and the use of an array of weapons, the most important being the sword. In the heat of battle, should the *katana* (long sword) have been lost or broken, the *samurai* had his *wakizashi* (short sword) and *tanto* (knife) as backups. If his only remaining weapon was his knife or if he had become disarmed, only then would hand-to-hand combat become important. As with the professional of any era, anything that enhanced the *samurai*'s chances of survival was crucial, thus systems of unarmed combat were not taught in isolation. These sub-systems of hand-to-hand techniques were known by a variety of names, such as Kumi Uchi, Yawara, Kempo, Taijitsu/Torite. Iizasu Choisai Ienao (1387–1488), the seventh grandmaster of the Muso Jikiden ryu (system), codified 100 unarmed techniques which he called Yawara Gi. The Takenouchi ryu, founded in 1525, included in its teachings a series of techniques called 'Kogusuku' or 'Koshi no mawari' ('around the waist').

One needs to remember that these were techniques executed by *samurai* in armour over equally armoured opponents. The focus, therefore, was on tactics such as holding and controlling an opponent with one hand so as to be able to stab him with a *tanto* without him being able to return the favour, or throwing the opponent to the ground. Any empty-handed striking would be directed to unprotected parts of an opponent's body — those that were not covered by armour. For instance, due to the need for mobility

around the shoulder joint, the armpit might have been a suitable target, and so the crux of the technique would have been getting access to it.

Whether these early techniques were wholly Japanese in origin, or influenced by Chinese methods introduced to Japan by monks and merchants, is of historical interest only. In the absence of written records, however, there is no way to prove their origin. Japanese culture has always borrowed, adapted and reverse-engineered liberally from its Chinese neighbour; and there is nothing quite as efficient as centuries of civil war to sort out which techniques are effective and which are not. Ones that were handed down by survivors were effective. Period. Even if their origin might have been Chinese, they were pressure-tested locally and the selection process was deadly.

The Tokugawa Shogunate, being a time of peace and harmony, had tremendous implications for the practice of all martial arts systems. Many teachers changed their focus of instruction from battlefield survival to character development. The execution of techniques was no longer restricted by armour. Since the pressure of an upcoming battle no longer existed, some teachers chose to specialize in a particular field. They would teach only unarmed combat or swordsmanship. For the first time, many of their students were not *samurai*, but merchants, craftsmen or peasants, who treated their martial arts training as a hobby.

Of course, some *samurai* families continued to hand down the traditional systems as practised in pre-Tokugawa Japan, from father to son, without any modifications, and some of these ryu can still be found today. These cultural heirlooms have great historical significance but little current applicability.

The rise of jiu jitsu

Historical records indicate that, in 1659, the Chinese monk Chen Juan Bin taught unarmed combat techniques to three *samurai* at the Shokokuji temple near Edo. These three founded new systems, each named after their founders: Fukuno ryu, Miura ryu and Isogai ryu. They strongly influenced other schools, such as the Kito ryu, which was a hybrid of the older Kumi-

Uchi methods and the newly acquired Chinese techniques. It was around this time that the term jiu jitsu was first used to describe these systems. Some of the more famous of these were the Jikishin ryu, Yoshin ryu, Kushin ryu, Sekiguchi ryu, Shibukawa ryu, Shin No Shindo ryu, Tenshin Shinyo ryu, Kito ryu and Yagyu Shingan ryu. A great diversity of techniques was practised, most schools specializing in one or other technical aspect. There was much rivalry between them and they guarded their secret techniques fanatically. Some still taught weapons' techniques, particularly the use of the sword. Due to the prestige and the economic advantages of being known as the best school, challenges and duels were frequent.

Towards the mid-1800s Japan's feudal system began to crumble and the trading nations of the world wanted greater access to a previously inaccessible Japan. Up until this time, Japan had been isolated from the rest of the world for two centuries. However, with the arrival of an American fleet and the opening of Japan to international trade, knowledge from the West streamed into the country. Thus everything foreign became immensely popular and traditional art and values were rejected. Jiu jitsu suffered from this trend as well. It was at this historically crucial time that a young man named Jigoro Kano took up the study of Tenshin Shinyo ryu with master, Fukuda Hachinosuke. After studying both the Tenshin Shinyo ryu and the Kito Ryu, he started his own school in 1882 at the age of 22, calling it the *Kodokan* and his system, judo. What differentiated Kano's teachings from most jiu jitsu systems at that time was an idealistic philosophy, a ranking system borrowed from Japanese sports, especially swimming, and the free-flowing sparring practice of *randori*.

What was clear was that jiu jitsu had not changed much in several hundred years and Kano revitalized the practice of Japanese unarmed combat. The opening up of Japan to the outside world saw to it that both jiu jitsu and judo became well known in international circles.

Between 1900 and the start of World War I, many masters who were skilled in both judo and jiu jitsu

techniques travelled around Europe and America. Some of the more famous exponents were Yukio Tani, Sada Kazu Uyenishi, Mitsuyo Maeda, Taro Miyake, Akhita Ohno and Gunji Koizumi. These early ambassadors popularized jiu jitsu extensively by taking on and beating all challengers. Tani, for instance, offered £20 to anyone he couldn't defeat in 15 minutes, and £100 to anyone who could defeat him. According to W.M. Bankier (*Jiu Jitsu — What it really is,* — published in 1906), Tani defeated an average of 20 men each week on a tour extending six months; a total of more than 500 challengers. As time went by, judo practitioners became more sports oriented. Many of the top judoka (practitioners of judo) neglected or rejected the practice of the judo kata (formal exercises), while jiu

Jiu jitsu and judo

There has been much discussion, especially since the popularization of Brazilian jiu jitsu, as to whether Brazilian jiu jitsu is actually a version of judo. Equally, there have been those who have claimed that judo, especially in its earlier years, was little more than jiu jitsu with ethics, a philosophy and a sporting aspect attached to it. Such arguments may be interesting but not necessarily pertinent. Judo today is an Olympic sport with a very specific set of rules, which determine what is allowed and what is not. Many of the techniques that are not allowed in judo are part of the Brazilian jiu jitsu syllabus, leg-locks being one example. Others, as practised for no-holds-barred matches, are closer to street-fighting methods than to a grappling sport such as judo. Of course, there are similarities between jiu jitsu and judo. The first generation of judo masters such as Saigo Shiro and Yokoyama Sakujiro, were originally jiu jitsu practitioners. The next generation of teachers such as Mitsuyo Maeda, who taught the Gracies, will in all probability have learnt techniques which originated at the Kodokan, as well as many from the older jiu jitsu ryu.

jitsu remained a collection of self-defence techniques, practised as such by the police force and military, as well as civilians.

Brazilian jiu jitsu

Mitsuyo Maeda, one of the early challenge-match specialists, settled in Brazil in 1915, where he attempted to establish a Japanese colony. Gāstao Gracie, a Brazilian of Scottish decent, helped him. Out of thankfulness for his help, Maeda taught Gastāo's son the art of jiu jitsu, who passed it on to his brothers, Helio, Oswaldo, Jorge and Gāstao. They, in turn, passed it on to their children and to many thousands of students.

Like Mitsuyo Maeda, the Gracies had an open challenge and were rarely beaten. Helio Gracie, for instance, was only beaten twice: once by top judoka Kimura and once by his own student, Valdemar Santana. Santana was beaten shortly thereafter by Carlson Gracie. One of Helio's sons, Rorion, brought the art to the USA and started teaching in his garage in Los Angeles. Brazilian jiu jitsu really took off worldwide when Rorion's brother, Royce, won the first Ultimate Fighting Championships, a no-holds-barred cage-fighting event, in 1994.

Since then, the Gracies have won many other such events, although in the last few years they lost occasionally against the likes of the Japanese professional wrestler, Sakuraba. This does not indicate that their techniques are no longer valid, but that everyone else is learning as much Brazilian jiu jitsu as they can and thus raising the standard of competition. Brazilian jiu jitsu's victory over many of the traditional kicking and punching arts such as Karate, Kung Fu and Taekwondo, has destroyed many cherished martial arts' myths, such that one deadly strike can kill or that high kicks are effective in real fighting situations.

As can be seen, jiu jitsu is an art of incredible diversity, both historically and in terms of its goals and technical content. It has something for everyone, and its emphasis on technique rather than strength makes it accessible and useful to men, women and children alike. Today's high crime rate provides a fertile ground for the art's continued growth.

above HELIO GRACIE HAS, IN HIS LIFETIME, ONLY BEEN BEATEN TWICE IN A CHALLENGE MATCH, THEREBY CONTRIBUTING TO BRAZILIAN JIU JITSU BEING THE FOREMOST MARTIAL ART IN RECENT HISTORY.

GETTING STARTED

In choosing a martial art and a school, there are many factors to take into consideration. Any real ability is the result of years of practice. This makes it incredibly important to choose wisely. There is nothing more likely to end involvement with a martial art than starting with one school, leaving after half a year because you realize this is not what you wanted, trying something else, and stopping because of frustration. Equally demotivating is sticking to a martial art for a year or two in the hope of learning to defend yourself, but becoming bored during the actual classes.

Goal setting

Goal setting is a skill that is as important in the martial arts as it is in life in general. The more specific your goal, the easier it is to reach it. Generalized goals are relatively useless. Wanting to get fit, for example, is a meaningless pursuit if it is not task-specific. What do you want to get fit for? The fitness of the long distance runner is very different from that of the powerlifter. To want to learn to defend yourself, on the other hand, is even more problematic because jiu jitsu claims to be one of the best self-defence systems available. This needs to be considered in some detail. Against whom do you want to defend yourself? An unarmed attacker? Is he a drunk in a bar, a mugger or a potential rapist? Similarly, what physical condition are you in to defend yourself and what are your chances of survival? Are you a police officer, a civilian, a man or a woman? How old are you? If you are older or with someone who for some reason can't run away, for instance, the 'flight' part of your 'fight-or-flight' decision falls away. What if your attacker has helpers, or what if he is armed and so are they? Defending yourself successfully against several armed assailants, without using a weapon and remaining uninjured, is nearly impossible in spite of what Hollywood would have us believe! Firstly, attackers don't queue up and attack one after the other, they usually all attack simultaneously. Secondly, contrary to the photographic sequences in most martial arts magazines, the attacker will not punch and then leave his arm hanging out there while you do a five-count countertechnique to his conveniently immobile body.

If your primary goal is self-defence expertise, you might want to ask a potential instructor if what he is teaching is useful in self-defence. Even more interesting would be to find out whether he has worked as a police officer or nightclub bouncer. Admittedly, many superb martial-arts stylists have never been in a single fight and this does not mean that they are not phenomenally skilled at their art. It does mean they have no first-hand experience of defending themselves in the kind of situation of which you are rightfully scared.

Self-defence and jiu jitsu

The recent no-holds-barred fighting events, although they are not street fights as such, are as close as you will hopefully ever get to seeing real fighting. What do these events show us? Not a single NHB (No holds Barred) fight has been won by a flying kick. No one has ever blocked any technique with a rigid classical block. Two or three fights have been won by roundhouse kicks but, statistically, for every one of these, there have been 99 others that were won by jiu jitsu chokes, armbars and leg locks. All these cage fights end up in the clinch and nearly all are finished on the ground. Eye gouging, biting and groin attacks are forbidden.

Any martial-arts technique will work on the street if the skill level of your opponent is low enough. Whom are you fighting? A biker in a bar is a much more dan-

opposite ALIVE SPARRING PRACTICE IS NECESSARY TO DEVELOP TIMING, SENSITIVITY AND DISTANCE APPRECIATION AND PROVIDES A STIMULATING CHANGE FROM COOPERATIVE TECHNIQUE PRACTICE.

gerous opponent than a pensioner with whom you are fighting over a parking spot. The main problem in a real fight is not knowing that you could or should claw at an opponent's eyes: most women who have tried to fight off rapists have probably instinctively tried to do so, but more often than not they are unsuccessful. The key lies in developing the ability to consistently get to the eyes in the chaos of a life-and-death struggle with a resisting opponent. The problem therefore is not the techniques in themselves (most martial arts include the eye gouge in their repertoire) but that most martial arts do not have a delivery system that encourages alive practice drills, done with a resisting practice partner, so as to make these techniques functional under pressure.

A good jiu jitsu school should have both preset training drills of a cooperative nature in which eye gouging, attacks to the throat and groin are practised, as well as free-flowing drills and sparring against resisting opponents. Preset training may work well in the street if you have the element of surprise on your side. Sparring and the alive practice of drills, on the other hand, are essential for when you are in body positions or situations that do not exactly match your idealized training. To provide one example: defences against grabs are usually practised in an upright manner. What if your attacker first pushes your head to such a degree that your natural alignment is completely broken? Your automatic response to this would be to regain alignment first, then to defend yourself. By that time, it may well be too late. If you have done a great deal of clinch and grappling sparring, you will have had the experience of being pushed and pulled in different ways. You would, with this background in training, find it relatively easy in this

situation to override the urge to stand up straight and convert your recovery movement to a level-change and take-down manoeuvre.

Too much sparring under limited rules can create its own set of problems. Many martial arts include punching to the head. This is fine if you are doing a specific sports form such as non-contact karate or a sport in which gloves are worn, such as kickboxing. Anyone with street-fighting experience will know that a hard punch to the skull is more likely to result in a broken hand than a knockout. Even 'Iron' Mike Tyson injured his hand in this manner in a street fight in New York. As far as punching to the facial area is concerned, this is also

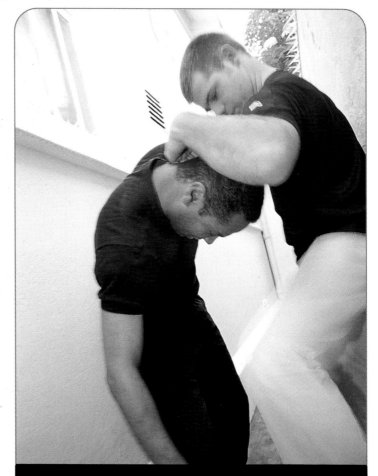

above SHOULD YOUR HEAD BE PUSHED DOWN IN A STREET FIGHT YOUR NATURAL ALIGNMENT WILL BE BROKEN AND YOU WILL BE VULNERABLE TO ATTACKS SUCH AS KNEE STRIKES TO THE FACE.

problematic. Impact to the forehead may lead to a damaged hand. Impact to the teeth may cause cuts on your punching hand, which in this day and age carries the risk of HIV infection. The nose is a good target, but situated where it is, between the teeth and the forehead, it may be risky on a moving opponent because you could miss your target. This leaves only the jaw as an ideal target for pre-emptive striking as it is easily dislocated or broken, as well as the chin which can lead to an instant knockout.

There are two observations here: when punching, the wrist often buckles under the pressure of impact, especially if you seldomly hit anything hard. In most jiu jitsu styles, if you must strike to the head, you would use a palm-heel strike instead. The slightly padded striking surface of your palm and its strong alignment with your forearm prevents damage to your hand. In addition, the palm's slightly yielding striking surface is not easily cut by teeth, and when cupped, is useful in breaking an attacker's eardrums. The hand formation of the palm-heel strike also converts easily and instantaneously to a follow-up grab for throwing or locking.

Again, if this strike is practised only in preset combinations on a cooperative training partner, there may be a problem in applying it in a chaotic, stressful real-life situation thus reiterating the need to train in an alive manner against a resisting, moving opponent so as to create a functional delivery system for your attacks. Sparring is one way of doing so and is necessary to develop attributes such as timing, accuracy, sensitivity (awareness of pressure) and awareness of distance, without which you would have problems applying your techniques. To this end, hand sparring with gloves that are heavily padded on the palm side would be optimal. Alternatively, you could opt for light sparring with no gloves using an open hand. (Remember to keep your wrist fairly loose and avoid accidentally poking your partner's eyes with your fingers.) Even boxing sparring would be ideal, as long as this does not lead to the counterproductive habit of striking to the head with the fist.

In jiu jitsu or judo, however, the preferred technique would be to hit an opponent with the largest striking

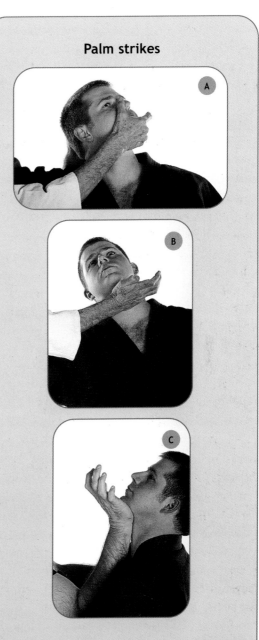

Palm strikes

(A) A palm-heel strike to the jaw or the side of the face can be converted into a double-handed throwing technique.
(B) The side of the palm can be used in a chopping motion to attack the windpipe. This is also sometimes known as a knife-hand strike.
(C) The upward palm-heel strike to the chin is used at extremely close quarters and converts easily to a follow-up eye gouge.

above DEFENCES AGAINST COMMON ATTACKS, SUCH AS THE DOUBLE-HANDED FRONTAL CHOKE SHOWN HERE, ARE A PART OF MOST JIU JITSU CLASSES.

surface available such as a floor or a wall, by the simple means of throwing him forcefully onto or into it. A skilful exponent can control the degree of damage caused to his opponent by changing the angle of his throw. He can either drop his opponent on his back or onto his head. In this instance, follow-up strikes are most often not necessary. No muss, no fuss.

Making your choice

A better understanding of the issues involved will allow you to ask a potential instructor questions. Ask to observe a class. In addition, any instructor who is not prepared to answer your polite questions does not have your best interests at heart.

In choosing your school, self-defence may, of course, not be your only concern. Long-time exponents often say that, if the only reason for studying were self-defence, you would be better off buying a weapon. Training can also be highly effective, but if it is incredibly boring, most students will not stay long enough to

reach any level of real proficiency. What often makes lessons fun is a martial art's sports aspect: its competitive training within certain rules. In Brazilian jiu jitsu, for instance, its most addictive aspect is the practice of sparring, known as rolling, which focuses on ground grappling and usually starts from a kneeling position. This becomes a game of physical chess, as a player does A, his partner counters with B, then the player counters that counter and so forth. Such practice is joyful, sweaty, energetic and, if one remembers to tap out when a submission is imminent, injury-free. At the same time, it teaches timing and sensitivity. Martial arts practice is a serious matter and yet, if there is no joy in the practice, it can become stale and repetitive.

Its sporting aspect also provides a large part of the fitness value of the art, further enhanced by movement exercises and supplementary sports-specific fitness training for the intermediate and advanced practitioner. Jiu jitsu, involving as it does pushing and pulling movements in all dimensions, works the muscles of the whole body in a very well rounded way, increasing both strength and flexibility. Depending on how energetic ally one plays the game (for instance, in ground-grap-pling one can play either in a fast-and-loose or slow-and-tight manner), cardiovascular fitness may also be enhanced significantly. You will not get very far, though, in fitness training as well as in self-defence if your training is effective but essentially boring where you are forced to run endless laps around a track, for example. If a part of you would rather be at home watching television, you will not achieve excellence.

There are other benefits as well. There is the social interaction with fellow practitioners, the prestige of climbing up the belt ladder and the sheer joy of a well-executed, well-timed technique. All of this begins with intelligent goal setting followed by visiting a variety of schools or clubs, asking questions and observing classes carefully. If possible, participate in a free trial lesson before signing up. Make sure that the teaching style and personality of the instructor appeal to you. The art is there to enrich your life; you are not there to merely perpetuate an art for another generation.

If you have set specific and achievable goals, visited enough schools and found one that fulfils your require-ments, then this could be the start of a life-long involvement in the martial art.

above SPARRING ON THE GROUND CAN BECOME A HIGHLY ENJOYABLE AND STRATEGIC SPORTS ACTIVITY.

Uniforms, belts and rankings

Jiu jitsu, with its great diversity of schools and styles, lacks any kind of uniformity with regard to uniforms, belts and rankings. In some schools street clothing is worn, tracksuits and T-shirts in others. More formal martial arts attire may include karate-type *gis*, judo *gis*, *hakamas* or Brazilian jiu jitsu *kimonos*.

There may or may not be a ranking system. Belts may be tied in a variety of ways. For instance, in Brazilian jiu jitsu the belt order is a fairly simple one. One starts with white, then blue, then purple, brown and, finally, black. There are various levels of black belt called dan in most Japanese systems and grau in Brazilian jiu

jitsu. Many styles have more coloured belts before one reaches black belt. Terminology may be expressed in English, Japanese or Brazilian Portuguese. Teachers may have formal titles or may be addressed by name.

In this incredible variety of options, the only thing of importance is how things are done in the school you have selected. The sheer diversity of styles makes it obvious that any claim made by a school that it is the only one to prescribe the correct uniform or have an ancient grading system is merely an opinion. Your fellow students and your instructor will be more than happy to inform you what the specific requirements are in your school and will help you fit in.

above BRAZILIAN JIU JITSU UNIFORMS ARE RECOGNIZED WORLDWIDE BY VIRTUE OF THEIR COLOURFUL MARKINGS AND PATCHES.

left ACHIEVING THE RANK OF BLACK BELT TAKES MANY YEARS OF PRACTICE WHILE MASTERY OF JIU JITSU IS THE RESULT OF A LIFETIME OF DEDICATION.

Basic Principles

The great diversity of jiu jitsu styles makes it difficult to create a conceptual structure that would apply equally to all of them. Classical *samurai* jiu jitsu as used on the battlefields of ancient Japan would not have included much ground grappling. A *samurai* in armour lying on his back with enemy soldiers standing, or on horseback, close to him would have made for an easy, less mobile target. Consequently, *samurai* spent a great deal of time learning how to avoid being thrown to the ground. In the Yagyu Shingen ryu, which has not changed much over many generations, escapes from throws included desperate tactics such as somersaults. This equates to modern hand-to-hand combat in the sense that the last place a bouncer or police officer wants to be is on the floor as his opponent's friends would probably use his head for target practice.

In times of warfare, sparring practice is less important than it is in times of peace. Skirmishes, ambushes and battles give combatants the opportunity to develop attributes such as timing, accuracy, sensitivity and distance-awareness. They are also able to pressure-test their technical skills since sparring with real weapons in this case is not practical.

Some basic principles in classical jiu jitsu can be outlined and their veracity will be recognized by those with sufficient combat experience. Jiu jitsu is an art that originated with professional warriors, not with farmers or peasants, and this shows in its conceptual structure.

Awareness

Awareness is the most basic skill required in combat and will most often determine whether you will survive a life-or-death situation. There are many stories of *samurai* who were so attuned to their environment that they could sense a hostile presence on a subconscious level before any of their five senses had picked up on this and their minds had coordinated it into a logical thought. An attack can either be a surprise (you are aware of it only when physical contact is made) or you are aware of it before it happens. The time period of this awareness may vary from hours to minutes to a split second before you are struck.

If a surprise attack consists of being grabbed, held, pushed or pulled, you should have a chance of regaining the initiative. If you are struck, and especially if a weapon is involved, you often have no defence.

Awareness, therefore, more than any specific technique, is the essential basis of combat jiu jitsu. It is the foundation of any warrior art and of living the way of the warrior. To the *samurai*, this awareness was reflected in fields as diverse as poetry, swordsmanship and lovemaking. Hence, also the *samurai's* affinity to Zen Buddhism, which emphasizes awareness and mindfulness. The more consistently aware the warrior is of his surroundings, the less chance he has of being attacked by surprise. Hypothetically, total awareness meant no surprises. Whether highly trained warriors or modern jiu jitsu practitioners, they always had a chance at a successful retaliation. Awareness leads to evaluation, which leads to decision-making beginning with the decision to either fight or flee. A surprise attack eliminates the flight option. Professional warriors sleep with their weapons close at hand and sleep lightly. It would be a safe bet to say that, in pre-Tokugawa Japan, there were few older *samurai* who were deep sleepers.

Jiu jitsu offers training that allows for faster and easier decision-making, and thus a faster reaction, to a threat. The various classical ryu had different tech-

niques for achieving this. A modern analogous example would be the use of a colour-code system as developed by expert combat shooter, Jeff Cooper. This system attempts to assist practitioners in attaining an all-pervasive awareness of their environment. Alert and switched on, individuals are said to go about their daily affairs in 'condition yellow'. As soon as they become aware of a possible problem, they switch to 'condition orange' and, as the problem becomes a reality, they move to 'condition red' and are ready to act on it. At this point, they are so primed to react that an onlooker may have difficulty in deciding who hit whom first. In combat, hesitation can be fatal. Thus if conflict cannot be avoided or evaded, it becomes necessary to be com-bat-ready as quickly as possible. This is the essence of a combatant's decision-making process.

Posture and breathing

Also of great importance in classical jiu jitsu is posture, stance and breathing. Under stress, be it in combat or when someone catches us unaware and makes a loud noise behind us, we exhibit what is sometimes referred

Subtle combat stances

The various types of subtle-combat stances taken up when facing an attacker should not give away the fact that you are a martial artist. These could take the form of:
(A) Covering most of your body with your arms, giving you the most defensive coverage possible.

(B) A stance you would adopt if you were an advanced practitioner and highly confident of your reaction speed.
(C) A stance you would take up if your attacker had a weapon. It is necessary and natural to extend your arms when faced by an armed attacker.

to as a startle reflex, a pattern of hunching up, contracting our muscles in anticipation of some sort of impact and holding our breath. Our hands may even come up to automatically ward off an anticipated blow. This is the last thing one would want to do in combat and is primarily a matter of not being caught by surprise in the first place. Posture and breathing also play an important role.

The next time you find yourself in a stressful situation such as heavy traffic or in an important meeting, focus on your breathing. Nothing complicated; just breathe deeply through your nose, imagining that you are pulling your breath down to your *hara* (belly). Notice what this achieves. Your muscles relax and your mind becomes clear. Similarly, should you be attacked, being tense would inhibit your smooth defence, thus deep breathing may counteract this. Being aware and in control of your breath is therefore just as useful for combat survival as it is for more common daily stressful situations.

As regards posture and stance, one of the greatest *samurai* swordsmen ever, Miyamoto Musashi, wrote: 'It is essential to make your ordinary stance your combat stance, and to make your combat stance your ordinary stance'. If you were attacked, and you first needed to set yourself in a complex and low classical martial-arts stance before you responded, your counterattack would be too late. Whether you like it or not, you need to react from whatever stance or posture you are in, particularly if you have been attacked by surprise. Thus, the more aware you are of an imminent attack, the more time you have to create a defensive position.

Even then, an overly exaggerated martial-arts stance is not recommended for a number of reasons. Why give an attacker the gift of knowing that you have some martial arts skill? If you sense that he is undecided; then taking up a threatening position may deter him, however, it is doubtful whether this will have the same effect on a potential rapist who perceives his victims to be smaller and weaker than himself.

When attacked, it would be better to adjust your standing position to a subtle combat stance by turning your body side-on to your attacker: feet shoulder-width apart, one leg ahead of the other. Most of your weight would be on your back leg; an even-weighted stance means you would first need to shift your weight

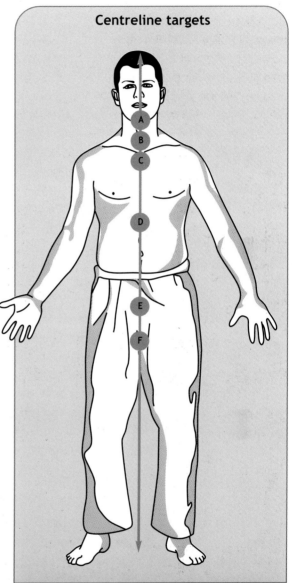

Centreline targets

MANY OF THE MOST VULNERABLE TARGETS ARE LOCATED ON A LINE RUNNING DOWN THE CENTRE OF THE BODY, USUALLY REFERRED TO AS THE CENTRELINE. THIS INCLUDES MORE OBVIOUS AREAS SUCH AS THE WINDPIPE (B) AND THE GROIN (F), AS WELL AS THE CHIN (A), STERNO-CLAVICULAR NOTCH (C); SOLAR PLEXUS (D) AND BLADDER (E).

on one foot before you could move, thus your defence would take twice as long. Slightly bend your knees, fold your arms across your chest, the arm closest to your opponent either resting on top of the other or folded across your chest, with the other raised vertically, thumb and forefinger on your chin. If you look at this posture from your attacker's perspective, he suddenly has very few obvious available targets. Other than your leading arm, he can no longer grab your chest, throat or head easily. He can strike, but striking targets on your centreline (imaginary line running down your front, from nose to chin to throat, solar plexus, bladder and groin) are not available. Targets for punching would be your leading arm and head, and since punching someone in the tricep or bicep would not occur to a street attacker, he would probably aim for your head. Should he attempt to tackle you, you could then choose to sprawl (see p58).

In the subtle combat stance, you are not open to sucker punches to the stomach, to surprise head-butts or knee strikes to the groin. With a fairly small adjustment of your arms and legs, you are thus able to put yourself into a coiled position of readiness and will have eliminated more than half of your opponent's attacking options. You have not taken up any position that could even be closely identified as a martial arts stance and yet the calm strength of your posture and your opponent's decreased number of attacking options may possibly lead to him having second thoughts about assaulting you.

Preparation

Very often an attacker may talk to you. This could take various forms and have several possible intentions. He may be psyching himself up for an attack, he may be trying to intimidate you or he may be trying to distract you for as long as it takes him to get into extreme close range of you, at which point you will be unable to respond timeously to an attack. (Many street thugs like to talk themselves into head-butting range.) If you were to allow him to come to within a few inches of your face, your reaction time would be too slow to respond to an attack. You have only two options: you

can either respond verbally or choose not to. There are those who may advocate warning attackers or requesting them to stop and desist. This is highly applicable to police officers, and may also help you defend yourself in court afterwards. In many combat jiu jitsu styles, however, practitioners are taught to say nothing; absolutely nothing. They offer no response whatsoever!

The attacker is basically conducting an interview. His verbal abuse is meant to 'psyche you out'. Your blank response should have the same effect on him, as he is expecting some sort of verbal response. By not responding at all to your attacker, he may feel as if a black hole has swallowed up his threats. This will certainly unsettle him and may cause him to look for a victim who responds in a way he is used to. This can be seen in ego-based violence between men where there is often a prescribed sequence of events that starts with challenging statements. The question 'Who do you think you're looking at?' progresses to insults and threats; then often one person initiates physical contact with a push, or by jabbing the other with a forefinger, and finally fists start flying. This process is reminiscent of two dogs barking at each other, working themselves up sufficiently so as to start tearing pieces out of one another. If one person simply does not play his assigned role, the whole process may well not take place in the first place. Nevertheless, in spite of this approach, an attacker may assault you anyway but he may lack his usual confidence and commitment. This response to verbal abuse works very powerfully in combination with the combat stance.

Pre-emptive striking

Attackers usually perceive themselves to be bigger, stronger or better armed than their victims. It is often said that the attacker sees himself as a predator such as a wolf and perceives his victim to be prey, or sheep. It may, therefore, not always be advisable to wait until the physical part of an assault has begun. A pre-emptive strike, as risky as it may be from a legal point of view, could be an option to consider.

The law pertaining to self-defence differs from country to country and every martial arts practitioner, regardless of style, should have a basic understanding of these laws as they exist in his country. This is especially important in pre-emptive striking, when you feel a threat posed by an attacker is sufficiently serious for you to attack him before he has actually struck you. The American saying that 'it is better to be judged by 12 than carried by six' applies in that it is better to find yourself in court, judged by a jury of 12, than to be carried to your grave. Having said this, once the immediate threat is no longer present, it is necessary for you to stop your attack.

Simplicity

Another core concept in jiu jitsu is simplicity. This is often referred to as KISS (Keep It Simple, Stupid). Research has shown that the higher the stress level, the more difficult it is to complete tasks that require fine motor skills. Catching someone's wrist in midair in a classroom setting is difficult enough (even if your fellow student is being very cooperative), but catching a fist on its way to breaking your jaw is nearly impossible. Something relatively simple, like ducking under the punch and doing a take down, is more effective. Kicking someone in the shin is possible; hitting an acupuncture point exactly three inches up from the xiphoid process on a moving target is not!

Remember that there is a crucial difference between a classroom setting and a street scenario; in the classroom you are practising with a training partner, while in the street you are reacting to an enemy who is intentionally trying to hurt you. Those who cannot comprehend the implications of this have simply not had much street experience.

These are some of the more basic concepts and principles of combat-oriented jiu jitsu. Applying these correctly would mean that the majority of your confrontations could be avoided and this, of course, is the ultimate self-defence solution. If you do not get into a fight, you cannot lose a fight, or, as one old jiu jitsu master put it: 'No-one ever wins a fight!'

above AN AWARENESS OF DANGER IN YOUR ENVIRONMENT MAY PREVENT YOU FROM BEING CAUGHT BY SURPRISE. ANOTHER WAY OF PREVENTING A SURPRISE ATTACK WOULD BE TO ENSURE THAT A STRANGER DOES NOT ENTER YOUR PERSONAL SPACE WITHOUT YOU PERMITTING IT.

CLASSICAL JIU JITSU

Basic and Intermediate Techniques

Despite the fact that there are several hundred different classical jiu jitsu styles in existence, ranging from medieval battlefield systems to modern eclectic sports grappling, there are certain commonalities that apply to all of them. There are, for instance, only so many ways in which you can lock an arm. Entries into an armbar vary from style to style; it may be done standing up or on the ground. There are, however, three basic ways in which an arm can be locked: it can be straightened, with pressure put on the elbow joint; or it can be bent upward or downward, with pressure exerted primarily on the shoulder.

Before illustrating the basic techniques of classical jiu jitsu, it is necessary to understand its core technical concepts. Jiu jitsu practitioners seek to gain control of their opponents. The closer you are to an opponent the easier it is to control him. The more control you can exert over him the better your chances are of making your technique work. If you can further restrict his options of movement by lying or sitting on top of him, or by skilfully pushing or pressing him into a wall, you increase your level of control significantly.

Even without a wall or the floor, your degree of control may often be an indication of the functionality of a technique or your skill level as a practitioner. Taking the standing armbar as an example: good technique means that you not only control your opponent's arm with your hands (one hand maintains a wristlock on the opponent, the other one presses the opponent's arm just above the elbow), you also control his body and movement options by bringing your body close to his. You support the armbar and, if possible, step through in such a way that one or both of your legs prevent your opponent from moving his feet.

Jiu jitsu consists mainly of close-range techniques. For a martial art to be effective it does not need to include thousands of movements or techniques executed at every possible fighting range. What it needs to have is answers to all the possible questions that may be asked of it in all possible scenarios. These could take the form of unpredictable street assaults or attacks by practitioners of another martial-arts style.

Jiu jitsu techniques that control opponents at close range rarely include long-range flying kicks as these are not functional, neither is boardbreaking or solo form *kata* (practice).

above A WRISTLOCK COMBINES WELL WITH A MORE ADVANCED COUNTERTECHNIQUE.

opposite IN EXECUTING AN ARMBAR, CORRECT BODY POSITIONING IS VITAL.

Technique categories
Atemi-Waza
(*Striking techniques*)

Striking techniques, including but not necessarily limited to, strikes with the hands (palm-heel strikes, hammer fists, knife-edge strikes, finger strikes and gouges), kicks, elbow techniques, knee strikes and head butts. The intended target is as important as the strike itself. A general rule-of-thumb for this is *hard tools to soft targets, soft tools to hard targets*. This implies that a punch to the floating ribs and a forearm strike (with the muscular part of the arm) or a palm-heel smash to the skull would be acceptable, whereas a hard punch to a hard target would not be.

Technique and target are vitally important. Being able to consistently connect the one with the other, especially under extremely stressful conditions, requires the kind of timing, distance-appreciation and accuracy that is the result of hundreds of hours of alive training with a resisting opponent.

Frontal-choke defence

⇗(A) The attacker is grabbing your throat with both hands and starting to exert pressure.

⇩(B) Secure his right hand with your left, twist your body and by doing so, set yourself up for an elbow counterstrike.

⇘(C) Execute an elbow strike to his jaw hinge. Your left hand maintains control of his right hand and is precisely placed to follow up with a wrist dislocation or wristlock.

Defence against strike
A swinging or looping punch, often referred to as a 'haymaker', is one of the most common forms of attack on the street.

⇦(A) Moving out of your chambered stance you turn your forearm out to intercept the force of his haymaker punch.

⇨(B) You immediately counter with a strike to his windpipe, using the area between your thumb and your index finger as a striking surface.

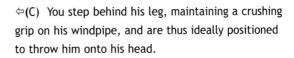

⇦(C) You step behind his leg, maintaining a crushing grip on his windpipe, and are thus ideally positioned to throw him onto his head.

Kansetsu-waza
(*Holds and Locks*)

Holds and locks, leverage techniques against joints. These methods may be used to merely control the opponent, as in a police officer arresting a resisting drunk, or as an attack against the joints, executed so as to tear ligaments and tendons. To clear up a common misconception: while it is not impossible to break someone's bones, it is difficult. Most Kansetsu-waza will tear the supporting structure around the joint rather than break the bones in two.

Defence against a bullying handshake
(A) As the attacker shakes your hand, he starts exerting undue pressure on it.
(B) Take the thumb of your other hand and place it against his thumb as indicated.
(C) Press his thumb inward and upward. The harder he grabs you, the quicker he will let go.

Small-circle wristlock
(A) As a basic training exercise for wristlocks, grab your cooperative training partner's hand.
(B) Using both your hands to secure his hand, immediately exert maximum pressure against his wrist joint.

(C) Maintaining the pressure, rotate his wrist upward into a better control position.

(D) Now exert pressure downward until his forearm is completely immobilized between your hands and the floor.

Hand-grab and step-through to lock

In a self-defence situation you would set this technique up with a pre-emptive strike.

⇨(A) Grab your opponent's left hand with your right hand as indicated.

⇨(B) Raise his arm as you step through under his armpit.

⇩(C) While rotating his hand start twisting his arm downward.

↘(D) Ensure that you maintain full control by twisting his arm as much as possible.

↘(E) You can finish the sequence by means of an armlock or a throwing technique.

Nage-waza
(*Throwing techniques and take downs*)

In any situation involving movement, our structure is well balanced in certain directions, and not so well in others. Since the ideal in jiu jitsu is to avoid using unnecessary force against force, this implies that a throw is preferably executed in the direction in which the opponent is not well balanced. The more committed the opponent's attack, the easier it is to determine the direction in which he should be thrown. If the opponent is skilled and remains well balanced, you need to unbalance him first so as to throw him. As you become more skilful, you learn to blend in with the attack by joining your centre to that of your opponent's (*see* p83), as if there is no resistance and you are the only one moving through space.

Types of throws may include throwing an opponent while remaining upright, as well as sacrifice throws. A sacrifice throw is one that entails you adhering to your opponent at the same time as either falling to the ground or rolling back, forcing him to follow.

In the more modern, eclectic jiu jitsu styles, wrestling take downs such as the single and double-leg take down, ankle picks and suplexes may also be used. The study of throwing implies that one needs to have a thorough working knowledge of breakfalls (*Ukemi-waza)*, otherwise one will spend more time injured than training on the mat.

Double-leg take down

⇦(A)   You are facing your opponent, who has taken up a posture that suggests some knowledge of boxing, so you decide to take the fight to the ground.

⇨(B) You throw a punch at his head so as to distract him and set up your take down.

⇨(C) You change levels, shoot in and control his hips by pushing into his stomach either with your shoulder or your head, simultaneously securing his legs with your hands.

⇦(D) Having positioned your hips underneath his and having upset the integrity of his structure, you raise his hips up. If he has a grappling background and you have placed your head next to his hip, you need to be aware of possible guillotine counters.

⇩(E) As you tip him over to the side, you immediately follow up by going to the mounted position. From here you follow up with strikes, chokes or armbars.

Shime-waza
(*Strangles and chokes*)

These may be aimed at cutting off blood flow to the brain by means of the carotid arteries, or may be aimed at compressing the windpipe. They are very dangerous, and even in practice, excess pressure on the artery and windpipe will cause long-term injury. In many of the sport forms of jiu jitsu attacks to the windpipe are forbidden. Sports-oriented practitioners therefore limit their chokes to compression of the carotids. Shime-waza can be executed by using the limbs only, without the use of clothing, as is the case with the rear-naked choke (*hadaka-jime* in Japanese, *mata leão* in Brazil) or the guillotine choke (*mae-hadaka-jime/guilhotina*). The legs can be used as in the triangle choke (*sangaku-jime/triangulo*). Shime-waza can also be applied using clothing, whether a *gi* (*kimono*) or a jacket in the street. In training, chokes should be released as soon as your training partner taps out, or when you suspect he has slipped into unconsciousness.

Defence against rear-naked strangle
⇧(A) You become aware that your attacker is about to apply a rear-naked strangle on you.

⇧(B) It is important to initiate your defence before he fully secures the strangle. Secure his arm firmly at the wrist and at the elbow.

↗(C) Turn your body as you start applying a figure-four armlock.

⇨(D) Twist his arm downward, exerting severe rotational pressure on his shoulder, and force him to the floor.
⇦(E) Maintain control of him by continuing to twist his arm.

Defence against frontal choke

⇧(A) The attacker grabs you by the throat.

⇧(B) You secure his right hand with your left hand and raise your other arm vertically. It is important that the arm is fully extended, your bicep next to your ear.

⬈(C) You twist your body and use your armpit to free yourself of the strangle. Then bring your elbow down to set up your elbow counterstrike.

⇩(E) Follow up with a wristlock and a possible knee strike to his face.

⬉(D) Execute an elbow strike to the side of his jaw.

Kyusho
(*Pressure-point attacks*)

The human body has certain areas known as pressure points that are sensitive to pressure and impact (*see illustration below*), but the degree of sensitivity may vary from person to person; adrenaline may reduce this sensitivity and drug abuse may eliminate it completely. A choke, on the other hand, works irrespective of the adrenaline levels or drug habits of the opponent. With a few exceptions, these pressure points tend to be small, and in an altercation may prove very hard to strike or reach.

Having said this, knowledge of where and how to inflict such pain may be useful in some self-defence situations in which the level of threat is not very high, namely when controlling a drunken friend at a party. It could also be used to momentarily distract an opponent prior to applying a strike, throw or lock. Occasionally, including pressure-point techniques in grappling or

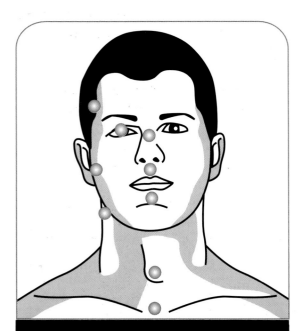

above THERE ARE MANY PRESSURE POINTS IN THE NECK AND FACE REGION. SOME TARGETS ARE ESPECIALLY USEFUL FOR STRIKING SUCH AS THE EYES AND THE WINDPIPE. OTHERS, SUCH AS THE CAROTID ARTERIES ARE BEST ATTACKED BY MEANS OF CHOKES.

sparring practice would be useful, but you should not base your combat strategy on this.

In practising and applying pressure-point attacks, you need to be careful. Certain choking techniques are potentially lethal and excessive impact to some pressure points may cause permanent damage. Be vigilant when executing them on a training partner. In the case of self defence, be knowledgeable of your country's laws and make sure that the force you exert corresponds to the severity of the threat or attack.

Technique combinations

Classical jiu jitsu techniques are seldomly executed on their own as it would be rare to execute a single move so well or with such speed that a *resisting* opponent would be defeated right away. It is common that techniques are used in combination, usually in accordance with the reactions of an opponent. Your assailant's reaction to your first technique will determine your follow-up technique. If you do have the element of surprise or if you are launching a pre-emptive strike, you may be able to apply such a technique perfectly; but even then it may be advisable to ensure your opponent is not capable of continuing his attack.

Possible combinations in jiu jitsu are endless. You could, for instance, strike, then throw, then strike again. You could also launch a series of strikes. Alternatively, you could strike, move in and execute a controlling hold, then throw and follow your opponent to the ground where you would continue the fight. This may not be a good option for the street if he has friends in the vicinity or if weapons are involved.

Do not preplan your combination techniques. It is important to stay mentally flexible so that you can adjust your combinations to your attacker's reactions. How he reacts determines how you will follow up. An exception would be a blitz of rapid headstrikes aimed at his vulnerable areas.

Be aware of the possibility of your opponent throwing a sucker punch with his other hand while he has you pinned in place by means of the handshake. Similarly, a head-butt is often preceded and set up by a double-handed chest grab.

Combination technique

↘(A) The attacker exerts undue pressure on your hand while shaking it and threatens you verbally.

⇦(B) You pivot step to his right side and secure his arm at the elbow with your free arm.

↗(C) You apply pressure to his wrist with your one hand and pressure to his elbow with your other arm.

↗(D) By utilizing his superior strength he manages to contract his bicep and escapes from your control. You follow his movement and flow into a downward figure-four shoulderlock.

⇩(E) He attempts to escape by straightening his arm. You allow him to do so and apply an armbar.

↘(F) As he bends his arm to avoid the pressure of the armbar, you transition into a hammerlock behind his back.

Defence against a rear bear hug

Being grabbed from the rear is more dangerous than being grabbed from the front. We are usually not very aware of the space immediately behind us and thus find it more difficult to defend ourselves if attacked in this manner.

⇦(A) Your attacker holds you in a bear hug from behind, pinning your arms to your sides.

⬉(B) You move your forearms, cupping his hands with your own so as to ensure that he is locked into position for your head-butt.

⬉(C) You contract your abdominal muscles and bend forward as much as his strength allows you to, so as to gather momentum for your rear head-butt. You snap the back of your head into his face.

⇨(D) The force with which he is holding you should now have decreased, allowing you to free one arm and shoulder by forcefully punching it downward toward the ground.

(E) You execute a rear-elbow strike to his groin.

(F) Step behind him with your leg and pull yourself smoothly out of his grasp.

In the case of a woman being attacked by a man, a series of several strikes would be recommended before attempting some form of controlling hold.

(G) Maintain your hold on his arm as you do so.

(H) Twist his arm behind his back in a hammerlock.

(I) You now have control over him and, if you so choose, can keep on forcing his arm up until the underlying structure of his shoulder starts tearing.

BRAZILIAN JIU JITSU
Principles and Movement

Brazilian jiu jitsu (BJJ), and other forms of sportive jiu jitsu, have become more popular in the last decade. This upsurge in popularity can be attributed to one family, the Gracies of Brazil. In 1801, Scotsman George Gracie settled in that country. His grandson, Gastao Gracie, became friends with Japanese judo and jiu jitsu expert, Mitsuyo Maeda, a fighter who won challenge matches against boxers, wrestlers and street fighters all over the world.

Maeda passed on his combative skills to Gastao's son, Carlos, over a period of six years. Carlos, in turn, passed on what he had learnt — one of his students being his younger brother, Helio, who subsequently changed the way in which many of the techniques were executed and taught. Because of his relatively small and wiry build, he relied completely on correct positioning and leverage instead of strength and athleticism.

Given fighters with evenly matched technical abilities, those who were bigger and stronger still won, but it became clear as the years went by that no one could equal the technical abilities of the Gracies, at least in Brazil. In challenge match after challenge match Helio defeated his opponents, using his superior technique to submit opponents much stronger than himself. Eventually opponents came from overseas to fight him and, after Helio defeated several Japanese *judoka*, he faced Masahiko Kimura, one of the greatest judo exponents of all time. In what was to be one of the only two challenge matches he would ever lose, the younger and heavier Kimura defeated Helio. His only other defeat occurred when, at the age of 50, he fought his 23-year-old student, Valdemar Santana, in a fight that lasted for nearly four hours.

Santana, in turn, was defeated by Carlson Gracie, son of Helio's brother Carlos, a year later. Both Helio and Carlos had many children and an incredible number of grandchildren. Since nearly every member of the family learnt the art of jiu jitsu and most became instructors, the art spread at a tremendous rate throughout Brazil. Between the 1920s and the early 1990s, various members of the Gracie clan and their students fought countless challenge matches known as Vale Tudo ('anything goes') and won nearly every single one of them, thus making the Gracies the foremost martial arts family in recent history.

In the 1980s Helio's son, Rorion, started teaching and popularizing the art in Los Angeles, California. He came up with the concept of creating a showcase for the superiority of BJJ, over most classical martial arts styles, by extending the challenge-match tradition that his family had so excelled in. This took the form of the Ultimate Fighting Championships (UFC), which was held in a large octagonal cage and televised. In it, a member of the Gracie family was pitted against various other stylists in an elimination tournament format. There were very few rules, eye gouging and biting being the main exclusions.

Rorion's brother, Royce, his wiry build reminiscent of his father's, convincingly won the first UFC. Since then, the Gracies and their students have won many matches in NHB competitions all over the world. As one Gracie family member has pointed out, even when they lost, their art won, as it is nearly impossible to win a modern NHB fight without a very thorough understanding of ground grappling as developed by the Gracies.

opposite BRAZILIAN JIU JITSU IS AN ENJOYABLE ART; A CONTEST OF SKILL IN WHICH TECHNIQUE AND LEVERAGE CAN BE USED TO SWIFTLY NULLIFY AN OPPONENT'S PHYSICAL ADVANTAGES SUCH AS SPEED, SIZE AND POWER.

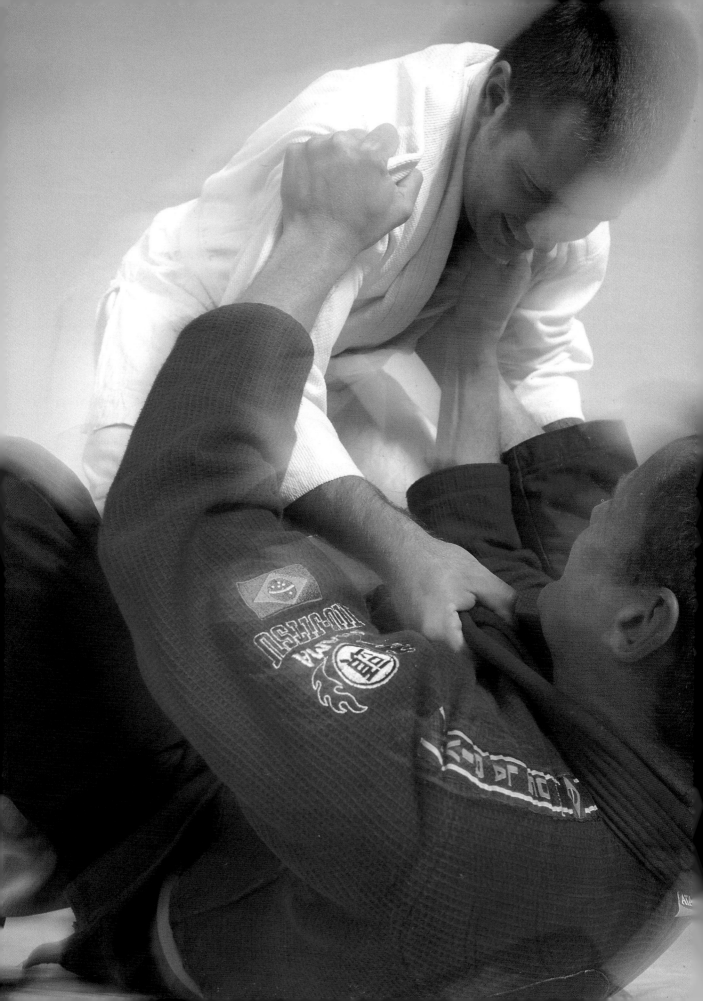

Why jiu jitsu fighters usually win

The question that arises is how and why the Brazilian jiu jitsu (BJJ) exponent nearly always seems to win, especially when facing opponents of stand-up fighting systems. The only group of fighters that has had any consistent success against BJJ fighters are free-style and Greco-Roman wrestlers who have added the Gracie ground-fighting game to their own repertoire.

After 10 years of evolution, the 21st-century NHB fighter will usually base his training and fighting strategy on a mixture of BJJ groundwork, wrestling take downs and clinchwork, with Muay Thai kicks, elbow- and knee-strikes as well as boxing punches thrown in for good measure. All of these four combat sports advocate practising in an alive fashion (against a resisting, moving opponent and with contact). While a top-level traditionalist from an art such as Taekwondo or Karate may theoretically be able to defeat a beginner or intermediate BJJ student, the record shows that such practitioners, when they have had the courage to enter the ring or cage with a good BJJ exponent, have been severely beaten.

For centuries these arts have been passed down and valued on the basis of their supposed deadly kicks, powerful punches and delayed death-touch pressure-point strikes. Yet, when it comes to an exponent facing a BJJ fighter in a challenge match, he or she fails miserably. Why should this be? The point is sometimes brought up that the stand-up fighter's deadliest techniques, such as eye strikes and groin attacks, are forbidden in these challenge matches. This argument might seem to hold some truth with regard to NHB sport matches that were televised in the USA or Europe (which excluded such tactics) but most challenge matches fought by the Gracies had no rules whatsoever. In both instances, the BJJ fighters won conclusively.

The reason for the effectiveness of BJJ is not just that it is practised in an alive manner, but also because of the specific tactics its fighters use. When a BJJ fighter faces a stand-up fighter, he will usually throw a few punches or low kicks so as to distract and capture his opponent's awareness. This gives the BJJ fighter a split-second of time to rush in and close the gap between them without getting hit or receiving more than a glancing blow from his opponent. As he closes the gap, his chin is tucked in, his head is lowered a little and his whole body is somewhat lowered as well. This makes his target areas (*see* p25) very difficult, if not impossible, to hit.

The opponent has two choices. He can stand his ground or he can retreat. If he chooses to stand his ground, he can throw one or two hand techniques or possibly kick once, before the fast-moving BJJ man is in the clinch with him and initiates a take down. If the opponent chooses not to stand and strike, but retreats instead, the situation is just as favourable for the BJJ exponent. With the opponent's legs and body weight moving backward, it is impossible for the stand-up fighter to throw any kind of hand technique with any power behind it. As long as the opponent is back-pedalling he cannot kick at all. Once he stops, the BJJ man is instantaneously on top of him because he can run forward faster than his opponent can retreat backward. The physics of the situation are thus that the opponent has very little chance of preventing the BJJ fighter from clinching and taking him to the ground.

Once on the ground, the situation becomes even more favourable for the BJJ man. A favourite BJJ saying goes: 'When we go to the ground, you are in my world. The ground is the ocean, I am the shark and most people don't even know how to swim.' Movement on the ground is utterly different from standing movement. The core muscles of the trunk, namely the muscles of the abdomen, lower back, pelvis and hips, power ground movement whereas standing movement comes from the legs. The BJJ fighter thus forces his opponents to fight on his terms, and unless they have taken extensive lessons in BJJ, once on the ground they become unskilled fighters and decades of training often turn out to be useless.

It could be said that BJJ mirrors the way in which animals fight in the wild. Whether it is a lion on the African veld or a wolf on the Siberian tundra, the predator charges in, latches onto its prey, drags it to the ground and kills it. The prey, whether elk, antelope or zebra, lashes out with its hooves, antlers or horns in a desperate and ineffective attempt to escape. As the Brazilians like to put it: 'Predators grapple, prey strike.'

All of this is not meant to imply that traditional stand-up martial arts are a waste of time. Hundreds of thousands of practitioners around the world today enjoy the health benefits, improved movement and self-discipline that these arts indubitably provide. It is simply that when it comes to two unarmed exponents with more or less equal training time fighting each other, the BJJ exponent will win with monotonous regularity. Many black belts in the traditional Oriental arts have thus taken up BJJ as a secondary study so as to improve their combat efficiency.

above IN VALE TUDO JIU JITSU, THE TECHNIQUES OF BRAZILIAN JIU JITSU ARE SMOOTHLY MERGED WITH THOSE OF COMBAT SPORTS SUCH AS BOXING, WRESTLING AND KICKBOXING. SUCH CROSS-TRAINING HAS RESULTED IN A REVITALIZATION OF THE CLASSICAL ART.

Rules and regulations

BJJ may have become popular because of its invincibility in NHB sports matches but a BJJ sports match is governed by a very complex set of rules and a very precise scoring system. In years gone by competitors worked strongly toward a victory by submitting an opponent by means of a lock or a choke. These days, with the increasing number of participants, prize money and the ability levels of the competitors rising every year, victory is often the result of implementing a winning strategy; of accumulating a points-lead at the end of a match. By not going for the big win by means of submission, exponents exposed themselves to less risk of losing, as it was often in the process of struggling to submit an opponent that their winning advantage was easily reversed.

This aversion to risk-taking behaviour led to a very stagnant, boring form of sport jiu jitsu in which fighters would often wait for their opponent to make a bad move so as to win by a narrow points lead. This situation has been changed by the introduction of the concept of an advantage. An advantage is scored when one fighter attempts a significant move so as to improve his position, but does not quite succeed in pulling it off. This naturally encourages fighters to take more risks and to attack more often.

If fighters have equal ability, a match can be an incredibly complex chess game in which victory goes to the fighter who briefly manages to achieve a superior position. If one fighter is clearly superior, he may choose to go for a submission (*see* p68) or else he may move from position to position, racking up points every time he makes a transition from one position of control to another. Bouts differ in length according to belt level. At blue-belt-level, matches are six minutes long, at black-belt level they last 10 minutes.

If one achieves a superior position or even submits an opponent whose skill level in BJJ is similar to one's own, then it becomes comparatively easy to do so when fighting someone on the ground who has little or no knowledge of BJJ.

The level of technical skill in Brazilian jiu jitsu matches has become so high that exponents often search for an advantage outside of the confines of BJJ. Thus, sports-specific weight training is becoming increasingly popular as is cross-training in other grappling styles such as Sambo, Greco-Roman or freestyle wrestling and judo.

Scoring

- A take down: two points
- Passing the guard: three points
- Sweeping the opponent: two points
- Achieving the knee-on-stomach position: two points
- Achieving the mounted position: four points
- Taking an opponent's back: four points
- Submitting an opponent by lock or by choke: automatic victory.

If a position cannot be securely held for at least three seconds it is scored as an advantage rather than producing full points. It must be remembered that the rules are continuously changing.

above THE MOST IMPORTANT SAFETY CONSIDERATION IN A SPORTING MATCH IS THE PARTICIPANT'S PREPAREDNESS TO TAP OUT AS SOON AS A HOLD, LOCK OR CHOKE HAS BEEN APPLIED.

above THE FLYING ARMBAR IS ONE OF THE MOST SPECTACULAR TECHNIQUES SEEN IN BRAZILIAN JIU JITSU. WHEN IT SUCCEEDS IT USUALLY DOES SO BECAUSE THE OPPONENT IS CAUGHT BY SURPRISE.

Movement on the ground

Grappling movements differ completely from movement on your feet. This is the fundamental reason why fighters with no ground experience behave like turtles turned over on their backs. Once a fight has been taken to the ground, their legs are no longer doing the work.

Moving forward, sideways and backward; ducking, bobbing and weaving; all movement in stand-up fighting is primarily achieved by the contraction and extension of the leg muscles, thus the use of the term 'footwork'. Rotating around your central axis, and coiling and uncoiling your body, may be vital for creating powerful impact when striking, but it is your legs that move you in relation to your opponent.

The core muscles of the trunk — the muscles of the back, abdomen, pelvic girdle and hips — power movement on the ground, and the hands and feet can be used to direct and assist movement. As such, they can be important contact points with the ground while the three-dimensional nature of movement on the ground means any part of the body can also be used as a contact point. To reiterate, the muscles of the arms and legs may enhance and support this movement with power and direction coming from the trunk, hips and the core of the body. If you are not familiar with and don't practise this type of movement, you will have problems should a fight go to the ground. It is highly recommended that the more basic movement patterns such as shrimping (*see* p49) and the Oopah (*see* p50) are practised solo before attempting to integrate them into technique practice or drills with a partner. If you cannot move smoothly and with control while moving on the ground on your own, how do you expect to move smoothly with a partner? Even if he is highly cooperative, you would still have to adjust yourself to his movement patterns and work with his body weight.

After the first UFC, when BJJ first became popular outside of Brazil, everyone was keen to learn its amazing submission techniques. It took a while before students realized that they are not too useful if an opponent has not been controlled; first you control your opponent, then you make him tap. To control an opponent you have to achieve a superior position. Realizing this, exponents started practising these positions.

The last and most overlooked fundamental piece of the BJJ puzzle is ground movement. It is, of course, possible to not work specifically on positions but to focus on submissions only; some Japanese shootfighters do just that. Successfully getting a submission then becomes a matter of luck. However, when you watch top BJJ fighters in both BJJ competitions and NHB matches, what strikes you is not only the control they have over their opponents but also the absolute control they have of their own ground movement patterns.

Some of these solo movements are based on BJJ techniques, others on *Bioginastica*, created by Orlando Cani, which fuses BJJ movements with Yoga, Tai Chi and animal-movement patterns. The foremost fighter of the Gracie clan, Rickson Gracie, studied this with Orlando Cani and so have many top BJJ exponents.

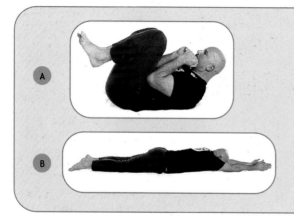

Extension and contraction

⇦(A) From the contracted, ball-shaped position, as shown, an infinite number of movements become possible. Each one of the four limbs can be moved separately or in conjunction with each other.

⇦(B) At full extension the body's potential for movement becomes severely limited. The more we resemble this configuration when an opponent has his body weight on top of us and controls our core, the less our chances of escape are.

It is truly amazing to see the infinite variety of ways in which the human body can move on the ground. Rolling forward; rolling backward over the shoulders and the upper back; flipping over from lying on one's back to a kneeling position; moving one's hips in various ways: these movement patterns are all highly applicable when escaping from inferior positions (*see* p60) or when maintaining a superior position with regard to one's opponent.

As difficult as it may be to adequately describe such complex movement, it boils down to the following: when you have your opponent stretched out to his full length on the floor, you can easily control him. He becomes like a wooden plank, and, as Jigoro Kano put it, a plank can be held steady under water by applying pressure on its centre point, or by exerting equal pressure on its four corners. When you are curled up into the shape of a ball, however, you are incredibly difficult to control. Any pressure that you interpret correctly (the attribute of sensitivity) can be countered by smoothly moving away from it.

Most core ground movements thus focus on your body's transition from a state of extension to either partial or full muscular contraction (wherein you are shaped like a ball), as well as all the given possibilities of movement within the three dimensions. When doing so, be aware of your breathing and posture. With sufficient practice you may understand these principles and learn to execute these basic movement patterns. This will also refine your movement in your daily life.

Shrimping

⇧(A) You are lying on your back, your feet drawn up as close to your body as possible.

⇧(B) Pushing off from the floor, raise your hips as high up as possible, creating the space underneath your body that you now utilize to move in.

⇧(C) Pushing firmly against the floor with one foot, move your weight onto the opposite shoulder and move your hips explosively backward. Push an imaginary mounted opponent's thigh away from you with your hand as you do so.

⇧(D) You should end up with your body in an L-shape. Now swing the body back into the same position as in A and execute the shrimping movement to the other side. This manoeuvre can be used to escape from the mount and the side mount.

Oopah

⇨(A) Lie on your back, your feet drawn up close to your body; your hands protecting your chest.

⇧(B) Raise your hips toward the ceiling forcefully. Work toward achieving as much height as possible. In application, the higher you can thrust, the more easily you can topple your mounted opponent off yourself.

⇧(C) Let all your weight roll onto one of your shoulders until you feel yourself toppling over to the side. As the Brazilian turn Oopah suggests, this whole movement has to be executed fluidly and explosively.

⇧(D) As your body turns and falls to the ground, make a point of drawing your knees forcefully in toward your chest. While you do so, specifically contract your abdominal muscles.

⇧(E) You should end up in a stable kneeling position. If you have used the Oopah to escape from being mounted, you will be in your opponent's guard, body upright, arms controlling his hips.

Kick and get up

⇧(A) This can be practised as a solo movement or it can be used to get up safely when faced by a standing opponent. You are sitting with your body angled sideways, and your hand is up to protect your face.

⇧(B) Putting all your weight on one foot and the opposite hand, raise your hips off the floor.

⇧(C) Rocking your body forward, use your unweighted leg to kick out at an imaginary opponent's shin.

⇧(D) Raising your hips high off the ground, pull the kicking leg through underneath you. The higher you raise your hips, the easier it becomes to move your leg through.

⇩(E) Move your leg back as far as possible to create as much distance as you can. Push off your front foot during the final phase of this movement to do so.

⇨(F) Come up into a fighting stance. From this position you can squat, execute a side breakfall and flow immediately into another repetition of this movement.

The Gracie strategy

BJJ uses a strategy developed by the Gracies that enables its exponents to achieve victory as intelligently and economically as possible. While this can be seen when they grapple with wrestlers, shootfighters and Sambo players, the strategy becomes most apparent in NHB or challenge matches in which the BJJ fighter faces someone with little or no ground grappling experience. In such matches, the BJJ man closes the gap, takes his opponent to the floor and then starts working his way from position to position, controlling him at all times. Once he has sufficiently restricted his opponent's movement options, he can proceed to lock a limb or choke him out at will. When the BJJ player takes his opponent to the floor — or if he is fighting against a good wrestler with superior take-down skills, in which case he may get taken to the floor — he will end up in a specific position relative to his opponent.

This position could be inferior, in the sense that he has no control over his opponent whose weight is on top of him, preventing him from getting the space he needs to work his way into a better position. The position could also be equally advantageous to both him and his opponent, enabling the fighter who is more knowledgeable and practised to use the position he has to move into, to effect either a superior position or a submission.

The guard position (see p65) is the best example of this. The fighter on guard has some control over the fighter on top of him by having his legs wrapped around his torso. The fighter on top, in turn, has a measure of control by using his body weight to pin his opponent down. If the fighter beneath the exponent, that is the one on guard, is technically superior, he can either execute a sweep (see opposite) or reversal so as to move into a superior position. Alternatively, he could submit the fighter who is 'in his guard' by means of a variety of submission techniques. If the fighter on top is the better player in a technical sense, or if he has better attributes, he could either 'pass the guard' (go past his opponent's legs), thereby moving into a superior side-control position or he could choose to submit his opponent by means of a leglock.

The position could also be superior. In this case, the BJJ exponent has some or all of his body weight stacked on his opponent. He controls his hips, which are preventing him from escaping, slowly and carefully tightening up his position so as to prevent his further movement. When the time is right, he could move to an even more advantageous position or go for a submission within that position. An example of this would be the so-called mounted position (see p61). To most BJJ players, this is the second best position to be in.

The Gracies have recorded most of their challenge matches on video. In most recordings we usually see the BJJ fighter achieving this position. Once he has done so, he secures it. Whatever the opponent beneath him does, the fighter mounted on top adjusts himself to it and maintains the mounted position, tightening it up further, and where possible, staying relaxed and responsive at all times. By remaining relaxed, he not only feels heavy to the fighter beneath him, he also gives him nothing solid to push against in his attempts to escape.

Implementing the game strategy, he hits his opponent, usually in the face, with an open hand rather than a fist. The hand formation presents less of a risk of injury to himself and transmits sufficient impact so as to elicit the desired response from his opponent, who may react in one of three ways. At first he may try to cover up, to shield his head and face with his forearms, but this will not work as there are too many gaps. Some force is also transferred to his head through his forearms. He may then either extend his arms in an attempt to fend off the blows or push against the chest of his tormentor. The moment he does this he is providing the BJJ exponent with a limb begging to be locked. The most commonly used submission technique under these circumstances is the straight armbar.

Alternatively, the man beneath the BJJ exponent desperately tries to escape the relentless face slaps and palm-heel strikes to his nose and mouth. He will do so by rolling over onto his stomach in the belief that this puts him in a safer position. The BJJ player gladly allows him the space and mobility to do so, since this is the worst possible position for him to be in.

Scissor sweep from the guard

⇩(A) Your opponent is in your closed guard. You have used your legs to pull him forwards, your left hand grabs his one arm, and the other grabs his *kimono* at neck level.

⇩(B) Open your guard, move your hips so as to get your knee in under his armpit until it lies diagonally across his chest.

⇧(C) Your other lower leg is positioned flat on the floor next to his leg and you are lying on your side. Push against his chest with your one leg while pulling in with your other leg, creating a scissoring action.

⇧(D) Your arms assist in pulling him over to the side. The main driving force comes not only from the hips but especially from the scissoring action of the legs.

⇨(E) The force generated by you, the momentum generated by your opponent's falling body and the connection between the two of you will have pulled you over and you will thus find yourself in the mounted position.

The fighter on top sinks in his hooks (hooks his legs under the legs of his opponent), secures the opponent's upper torso, extends his own body so as to straighten the opponent out, painfully pinning him to the floor with his hips. Now it is completely up to the BJJ exponent to finish the fight in whichever way he chooses. If he is in a street fight he could simply strike the back of his opponent's neck and the base of his skull, or he could smash his face repeatedly into the floor. However, the more elegant and economical finish would be the rear naked strangle (*see* p77).

This strategy might take a little more time to implement against a fellow grappler but against someone who has limited or no experience fighting on the ground it is frighteningly effective. This strategy is still being constantly refined and updated as fighters world-wide learn its details. The Brazilians consistently streamline it, taking new developments into consideration. The latest version owes much to the techniques and concepts developed by the so-called Brazilian Top Team (BTT), a stable of fighters led by Mario Sperry and Murillo Bustamente.

The ease with which BJJ exponents have dominated their opponents has created a polarized response on the part of traditionalists and stand-up fighters. While some have become enthusiastic students of BJJ, the majority have gone into denial. They claim that, all evidence to the contrary, if they were ever to fight against a BJJ player they would defeat him by means of their deadly eye-strikes and groin attacks.

above IN CHALLENGE MATCHES OF THE GRACIES THE REAR-MOUNTED POSITION, WOULD BE THE PREFERRED OUTCOME.

Hip heist from the guard

⇧(A) Another possible sweep that you can use to get from being 'on guard' to the mounted position is the hip heist.

⇩(C) Pushing off from the floor, punch your hip up towards the ceiling. The positioning of your body will convert this thrust to a circular movement and the way in which your opponent is held by your arm and the thrusting hip ensures that he will be swept over onto his back.

⇧(B) Open your guard by uncrossing your ankles. Move your hips back a little and sit up, supporting the weight of your upper body on one elbow. Position the other arm over his back.

Another possible response to finding yourself 'on guard' would be to scoot your hips backward away from your opponent, while pushing him away with your arms and either coming up onto your knees or standing up.

⇩(D) You will find yourself in the mounted position and can now initiate your attack from there.

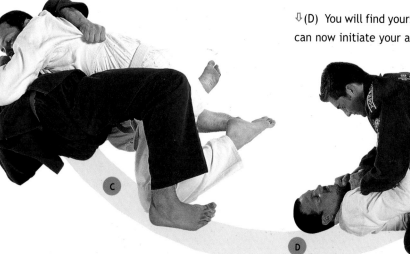

Vale Tudo: Neck-control drill

⇐(A) This drill teaches you to attain the neck-control position, in which you manipulate your opponent by having both your hands around his neck or placed on the back of his head. Start up with one hand around your opponent's neck, the other one either on his scapula or grabbing his triceps.

↗(B) Alternating with your opponent, thread your outside arm in under the arm he is using to control your neck. This gives you two-handed control.

⇓(C) He then, in turn, threads his arms in, one after the other, to achieve control of your neck.

↘(D) The first few times you do this, you practise cooperatively. Once you have understood the drill, you abandon any sequence and attempt to prevent your training partner from gaining access. Start moving around by adding footwork and use the phase in which you control his neck to pull his body around, using your body weight to do so.

Basic principles

There are many principles and concepts in BJJ, some basic, some more advanced. An understanding of these will provide a good foundation for improving your game. Some have already been covered, such as the importance of movement. Other core principles are:

Control

In BJJ you learn to control your own movement first. You then learn how to control your opponent and his movement. Without attaining control, victory becomes a matter of luck. With it, it is only a matter of time before you win. You need to control your opponent while you are working towards a superior position. It is also important to do so as you move from one position to another, to set up your technique and to execute it.

Space

If you are in a superior position, you slowly tighten it up, by eliminating whatever space your opponent may have in which to move. Like an anaconda, you wrap

above USING OPEN-GUARD VARIATIONS SUCH AS THE DE LA RIVA AND SPIDER GUARD, THE PLAYER AT THE BOTTOM HAS INCREDIBLE CONTROL OVER THE OPPONENT ON TOP.

yourself tighter around him until he is immobile. You pull him into yourself by means of your arms.

If you find yourself in an inferior position, it is quite likely that your opponent is your technical equal if not your superior. You then need to create space so as to move. You do so mainly by moving your hips, although you can also use your forearms, hands, knees and feet.

Weight

If you are in a superior position you can use your weight to pin your opponent down and immobilize him. To this end, you would focus and direct your weight by pulling him in with your arms and pushing into him with your feet. As in Jigoro Kano's analogy, weight can act as a single spike pinning an opponent down at his centre. Alternatively, it can be spread out so as to cover him like a wet blanket. As your opponent attempts to move one of his shoulders or hips, you shift some extra weight there so as to counter him. If you find yourself in an inferior position, you need to get out from under this weight, and you can do so by executing explosive and continuous hip movements.

Leverage

The use of leverage in BJJ is what makes the martial art so unique and different from other ground grappling systems. Successful application of BJJ techniques is not a matter of size, strength and speed but rather of correctly applied leverage. Holding a *gi* or *kimono* in different ways helps to nullify a larger player's strength and a smaller player's speed and mobility, thereby leaving them no option but to compete on the basis of technique, sensitivity and timing.

Sensitivity

In BJJ, sensitivity is the awareness of pressure (you cannot be aware of pressure if you are tense). Relaxing your body is one way of accurately reading your opponent's intentions; go along with it, join your centre to his (*see* p83) and then direct the movement.

The sprawl and other defences against throws and take downs, such as the underhook used in the clinch, are vitally important, especially if you prefer to fight in the stand-up ranges or when fighting someone who is a better grappler than yourself. To achieve excellence in these techniques, practise with training partners who have freestyle and Greco-Roman wrestling backgrounds.

Sprawl defence against a take down

(A) You are facing your opponent, he moves in on you and starts to execute a level change.

(B) As he attempts to control and move your hips backward 'punch' your hip bone at him by thrusting your hips forward.

(C) At the same time, throw your legs back. His forward momentum thus dissipates and your body weight starts to push him down.

(D) You are now lying on top of him. If his take down was not forceful, you could be on the balls of your feet thus giving you greater mobility to move around him. If it was forceful it may be necessary to point your toes away from yourself as you throw your legs back and out. His force will thus dissipate by him pushing your body along the tops of your feet. After you find yourself on top of him, you can 'helicopter spin' on his back, aligning your body with his and setting yourself up to execute the rear naked strangle.

Timing

Timing is the ability to identify a window of opportunity and to use it. One of the main differences between a purple-belt and a black-belt practitioner in BJJ is their timing. It takes many years of practice to reach purple-belt level, but those who do, know most BJJ techniques but will not have the black-belt's timing.

Only alive sparring (rolling) done with sensitivity and awareness over thousands of hours will develop timing. Without this experience, one is forced to apply brute strength in an attempt to open a window of opportunity. The use of such brute strength, in turn, leaves one vulnerable to an opponent's counters.

Defence first

Most beginners want to learn offence; a wide range of exciting submission techniques. While this may seem like a fun thing to do, if your defence (your bottom game) is weak, you are forever in the position of someone who is fighting with his back to a precipice. You know you must achieve a superior position, otherwise you are in trouble. This could cause you to tense up which will render you unable to play with sensitivity, giving you no option but to work with size, strength and speed. This may cause your game to stagnate and your abilities may never develop.

If you have a superb bottom game, however, your opponent cannot control or pin you down for any length of time and thus you have nothing to be afraid of. You are confident. This allows you to take risks and to grow. Confidence enables you to relax. Being relaxed, you move with sensitivity and economy of movement. This also means that you are giving your opponent very little that he can move or work against. How can he control you if he has nothing to move against? The two most essential skills that a beginner should work on, if he wishes to excel in time, are to attain full control over his movements and to develop his bottom game.

These are by no means all the principles of Brazilian jiu jitsu but they are the most basic and important ones. As in most martial arts you will find that the correct application of basic principles is much more important than learning advanced principles, most of which are only applicable occasionally.

above IN PASSING THE GUARD IT IS IMPORTANT TO KEEP YOUR WEIGHT STACKED ON YOUR OPPONENT SO AS TO COMPLETELY IMMOBILIZE HIM.

The positions

There is no agreement as to the exact number of positions in Brazilian jiu jitsu, as some of them can be categorized as single entities or are subdivided further.

With the ongoing evolution of BJJ, some positions are expanded or take on new significance. A good example of this would be the half guard (*see* p64) which previously was used more as a point of transition rather than a position in its own right. Recently some top BJJ competitors in Brazil developed the half guard into a strong attacking position and have since consistently won by applying submissions from it. In accordance with this, the scoring system has been changed, making the half guard a valuable position in its own right.

The way BJJ classifies its positions is by sorting them into superior, inferior or equal positions. Accordingly we speak of a top game (gaining, maintaining and utilizing a superior position), a bottom game (escaping from an inferior position) and a guard game (attacking and defending from 'in the guard' or from being 'on guard').

Rear Mount
Superior position

This is the most advantageous position in BJJ. Since your opponent is facing away from you, he cannot attack you in any way. If you have your 'hooks in' (grapevining your opponent's legs with yours) and have straightened him out, sandwiched between you and the floor, his movement options are nearly non existent. You have won the fight, unless you make any serious mistakes, such as letting him come back up on his knees while you are paying too much attention to applying the rear naked strangle.

Inferior position

Once you have been flattened out and your opponent is secure on your back, the fight is probably over. Your movement options are limited. You can turn around to get back to being mounted or, preferably, as he is trying to get his 'hooks in' or when he goes for the strangle, you roll over your shoulder and twist your body around as you do so. If you succeed in doing this you will find yourself in his guard (*see* p65). Should you still not be able to achieve this, he will still have your back and there is still the threat of being strangled. Nevertheless, you have more freedom to move since he no longer has you pinned between himself and the floor.

The Mount
Superior position

This position is the same one used by every schoolyard bully in the world. Your opponent is flat on his back and you are sitting on his chest, your knees on either side of him. You can lie flat on top of him, grapevining, which is very uncomfortable for him and prevents him from using his legs or hips to initiate the movement needed to escape. You can ride on top of him with your body upright, sitting at the level of his solar plexus, or you can push your knees up under his armpits to achieve the so-called high mount. This severely limits his ability to freely move his arms and leaves them exposed to your submission attacks. Unless it's a sport BJJ match, you may opt to strike him. Your hands can reach his face but his cannot reach yours. You can choke him out or you can submit him with an armlock (*see* p71, p73) or an armbar (*see* p29, p72). With practice, and by staying relaxed, it is fairly easy to counter the movements of the inexperienced opponent beneath you.

Inferior position

This is not a very good position for you to be in, flat on your back, pinned down by your opponent's highly mobile weight. If you lack knowledge and experience, you may not be able to escape. If you have three or four well-rehearsed escape techniques specific to this position at your disposal, you may have a chance to escape by grouping them together and executing them at speed. You could do so without creating a set pattern, hoping that somewhere in this sequence you are moving in a direction that your opponent has not blocked (since he may be coping with the final phase of the previous escape technique you have attempted).

Side Control

Superior position

There are several positions that can be grouped together in this category. There is the classic BJJ side mount, also called the 'hundred kilos' (so called because it feels as if there are 100 kilograms on your chest) in which you have your weight on top of your opponent's chest at a 90-degree angle. Some fighters base their attacking game on this position, others like to treat it as a transitory stage on the way to attaining the full mounted position.

The knee-ride or knee-on-belly position (*see* p63) is a superb side-control position. One knee is pressed into the opponent's belly and the other leg may extend out to the side acting as a rudder. The arms are used to further secure the position by holding onto the opponent's arms or neck. It is a superb position not only because it is extremely painful to the opponent and good for striking, but also because you can instantaneously transition to a standing position. This is particularly useful should you be using this in a street self-defence situation wherein someone could come to your opponent's

assistance. Also, this position allows for equal access to chokes, armlocks and leglocks. In the mount, for example, leglocks are not an option.

The scarf-hold position (*see* p63) tends to favour large, heavy fighters. In this position, you secure your opponent's head with an arm and use your other arm to clamp his arm against your ribs and under your armpit. From here, you can either apply a neck-crank or choke, or lock his clamped arm. Given more or less equal weight, a knowledgeable opponent may be able to work his way out of this position far more easily than out of a well-secured side-mount, for example.

The last side-control position worth mentioning is the '69' position (*see* p63). Seen from above, both bodies form one straight line with a set of feet at either end of it. Your chest or solar plexus is pressing into your opponent's face or the side of his head, making breathing very uncomfortable for him. This position is usually used as a hold-down or as a transition point when moving from one side-control position (on the side of your opponent's body) to another and it is not a major attacking position.

Inferior position

Escaping from a side-control position may be slightly easier than escaping from being mounted or rear-mounted. As always, this depends on your skill level as compared to that of your opponent's. If he attempts to achieve side-control after passing your guard, it is extremely important to prevent him from flattening you out on your back. If you can stay somewhat side-on to him with your knees drawn up and your top arm warding him off (the ball shape again), you are halfway to having escaped his control. If he does flatten you out, use your forearms as a barrier or bumper to allow you a little extra space to move. You do not want direct chest-to-chest contact.

Knee-on-belly Position

In all escape attempts it is important to remember that you need to start escaping the moment you are put into this inferior position. You cannot rest for a few seconds to catch your breath since your opponent will use this to secure his advantage. The more he establishes his position and tightens it up, the less likely you are to escape. The specific escape technique you attempt depends entirely on how your opponent is placed. Where is he putting his weight? Where are his arms? In which direction can you move your hips?

Scarf-hold Position

'69' Position

Half Guard
Superior position

You are on top of your opponent, he has both of his legs wrapped around one of yours. You are halfway between being in his guard and having him in the side mount. In this case, armlocks may be the best techniques to apply from this position.

Inferior position

You are underneath your opponent, your legs are wrapped around one of his. He will be trying to submit you or to free his trapped leg to transition to the mount. The most common response would be to not let him free his leg and to place him inside your guard.

On Guard
Equal position

You are on your back and your opponent is between your legs. If you have crossed your legs at your ankles behind his back, this is called a closed guard. If your legs are open, this is called an open guard. There are many variations to it, with exotic names such as spider guard and De La Riva guard (named after a great champion, Ricardo de la Riva). You can use your legs and feet to control your opponent, and while this may at first glance not appear to be an advantageous position to be in, it's not the case, as you have a wide range of retaliatory options.

If you are a good guard player you would attack continuously from the guard. You may try to secure an arm and effect an armlock or a triangle choke, a Kimura shoulderlock or a guillotine choke. Alternatively, you may attempt to sweep your opponent (reverse the situation as to who is on top). If you succeed you may end up mounted on your opponent. You could also scoot out of the guard position, come up on your knees and attack from there. Only a BJJ beginner will drop flat on his whole back, encircle his opponent with his legs,

cross them at the ankles (closed guard) and hang on for dear life. An intermediate or advanced player will use the open guard and attack from it.

The guard is probably the key position in BJJ. Players spend more time in this position than in any other and it is technically the most complex of positions. The often relatively slender Brazilians, when faced by some of the large and extremely muscular American wrestlers such as Mark Kerr, Mark Coleman, Tom Erickson and Dan Severn, had no choice in being taken down to the floor by means of the wrestler's single- and double-leg take downs. The wrestler, who according to the rules of his sport achieved his purpose (pinned his opponent's shoulders to the mat), was usually at a loss with regard to what to do next. He would usually opt for ground-and-pound tactics, punching and headbutting his opponent in whose guard he was. By doing so, he would often play straight into the BJJ exponent's hands (an arm fully extended for a punch is a tempting target for an armbar submission to someone who has been practising such techniques all his life).

In the Guard
Equal position

You are standing or kneeling between your opponent's legs. You may attempt a leglock on one of these legs but, to do so successfully, you need to have superior leglocking skills (as you are not starting off from a position in which you have extensive control over your opponent). In other words, if your opponent is fairly experienced, you may initially control his leg or foot but not at the end of the technique. Alternatively, he may also grab your leg and attempt a leglock while you attempt yours.

If it's an NHB match, you may opt for ground-and-pound tactics. A safer option would be to pass his guard (to move under, over or past his legs so as to achieve a superior side-control position). When two experienced BJJ players face each other on the mat, this guard game can become as complex and as subtle an exchange as that between Olympic fencers or chess grandmasters. Both men know their own moves and the moves their opponent is likely to make. Move, countermove and feint follow with split-second timing and sometimes a full 10-minute match can pass in this position without any positional change (with victory going to the player who may have come close to effecting one pass or securing a submission).

These, then, are the main positions of BJJ; the main intersections on the highways of BJJ movement. Wherever you are relative to your opponent, you are always only a few inches away from executing one of these positions: you move into the nearest position, you are then in a familiar place and you start working from there. Eventually, after many years of rolling with other BJJ players, every position in which you find yourself is one in which you have been thousands of times before. It is at this point that you may transcend the need for gameplans; you move freely and in accordance with the needs of the situation.

Open guard

Closed guard

Common escapes

Escape from being mounted

⇦(A) This is essentially the Oopah movement applied against a mounted opponent.

⬀(B) Secure his *kimono* at the wrist with one hand and use your other hand to further secure his arm above his elbow. On the same side on which you have secured his arm, pin his leg with your foot, preventing him from posting his leg out when you bridge him off yourself.

⬆(C) Thrust your hips toward the ceiling as high and as forcefully as you can and, by pushing against the floor with one foot, tilt onto the shoulder on the side on which you have controlled your opponent's limbs.

⇦(D) Allow yourself to roll over that shoulder and you will find yourself in your opponent's guard.

Escape from side control

⇩ (A) This is one application of the shrimping movement. Your opponent has the side-mount on you. Ensure you are using your forearms to give yourself some freedom of movement under his weight.

⇩ (B) Raise your hips off the ground. This creates space underneath you in which, and through which, you can now move.

⇩ (D) As you do so, you create space between yourself and his torso.

⇧ (C) Scoot your hips out sideways.

⇩ (E) Bring your knee into this space, as high up against your own chest as possible.

⇘ (F) Pivot your hips inward by 90 degrees, and adjust your legs, putting your opponent in your guard.

TECHNICAL SKILLS

Submission Techniques

Submission techniques are used in BJJ to make an opponent acknowledge his defeat by signalling through 'tapping out', using his hand to either slap the mat or his opponent's body or verbally requesting the match to be stopped. Though submissions may technically be similar, or at times even identical, to classical jiu jitsu joint and neck attacks, the BJJ sporting philosophy implies they are used differently. The aim of jiu jitsu within a sporting context is to dominate your opponent within given rules whereas the aim of classical jiu jitsu is to survive a potentially deadly encounter.

In a sporting match you might use an 'Achilles tendon' leglock to cause your opponent to signal submission. In a street encounter it might make more sense to use a technically similar, but potentially much more damaging 'heelhook' leglock, to seriously damage your attacker's knee. If the ligaments supporting his knee have been torn, it would be impossible for him to pursue you as you escape.

It might be said that classical jiu jitsu concerns itself with mutilation while sport jiu jitsu focuses on domination; this applies to the sporting aspect of BJJ as it does equally to other sport jiu jitsu systems. The ultimate expression of this domination is by means of the submission technique.

Most BJJ submission techniques, if applied with speed, determination and through their full range of motion, could potentially be used to injure an attacker in a street fight. Once combined, their possible permutations are endless, particularly since their execution within a sports setting has to take an often equally skilled opponent's countermoves into consideration.

Basic submission techniques

Although there is some variation as to which submission techniques are taught first, the 10 basic submissions on the following page would be in a beginner's syllabus in most schools. Leglocks would be taught last and there are some schools in which they are only taught at an intermediate level. While it is possible to teach submissions from the first lesson onward, you could quite easily and profitably spend your first half-year learning movement and position only.

Learning and attempting to apply submissions at too early a stage in the learning process usually results in a beginner's game lacking fluidity as his tendency will be to try to spot an opportunity to submit his training partner. His awareness will be focused on victory and on scoring points rather than on his movement, breath, flow, control of body movement and position, and as a result, his rate of progress could be slow.

above SUBMISSION TECHNIQUES ARE BASED ON GOOD POSITIONING SKILLS.

opposite CARE SHOULD BE TAKEN WHENEVER PRACTISING NECK AND FACE CRANKS WITH YOUR TRAINING PARTNER.

Straight armbar from the mount

The straight armbar from the mount is probably the second most often used technique in challenge matches between the Gracies and their traditionalist opponents. Against an experienced grappler it may be risky as, once you start the movement, you are fully committed to it.

⇨(B) You frame his arm with your hands, rock your weight forward until your arms are supporting it, thereby allowing your body to move freely. Kick both legs out and spin so that you end up at a 90-degree angle to him.

⇧(A) You are in the mount. Your opponent either pushes against your chest or face, thereby giving you a straight arm.

(C) Keeping your buttocks as close to your opponent's shoulder as possible, you drop back, his straight arm clamped between your thighs. Your knees squeeze together tightly to secure the technique; you make sure his thumb is pointing up so as to have his elbow aligned correctly.

(D) Raise your hips upward until the pressure on the elbow makes him tap out.

Figure-four armlock from the mount

This is a less risky technique than the straight armbar, as your body stays on top of your opponent and in full control of him. Should you need to abandon the technique halfway through executing it, you are still in your superior position.

⇧(A) You are in the mount. Your opponent protects his face with his forearms.

⇨(B) Your right hand grabs your opponent's right wrist.

⇨(C) You drive his arm to the floor.

> *Once you have achieved the mount, you might pretend to initiate one type of attack such as a choke, and once you have captured your opponent's awareness with this, swiftly change to an armlock.*

⇨(D) Slide your other arm under your opponent's arm and grab your own wrist.

⇩(E) Keeping your weight on your right elbow, pull his elbow up off the floor and towards his own feet, with the back of his hand moving on the floor as if it were a paintbrush (*see* F).

Straight armbar from the guard

The guard position makes the BJJ beginner feel extremely vulnerable. Until you have learnt techniques such as the armbar, Kimura, triangle choke and sweeps, you will feel helpless but once you can implement them with ease, the guard may end up being one of your preferred positions, especially in sporting contests.

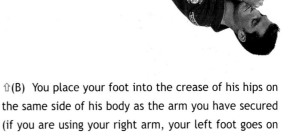

⇧(A) You (blue) have him inside your guard. You hold one of your opponent's arms and pull it diagonally across your chest.

⇧(B) You place your foot into the crease of his hips on the same side of his body as the arm you have secured (if you are using your right arm, your left foot goes on your opponent's right hip).

⇧(C) Move your legs and torso into a 90-degree angle to his body and bring your other leg up under his armpit, while maintaining pressure on his torso.

⇧(D) Remove the leg from your opponent's hip, push his head down.

⇦(E) Bring your leg over his head.

⇨(F) Squeeze your knees together to secure your opponent's elbow; make sure your thumb is pointing up, and lift your hips.

Kimura armlock from the guard

The Kimura works well in combination with techniques such as the hip-heist sweep and the guillotine choke from the guard. In each of these three techniques you come up onto one elbow to set it up. From there it becomes relatively easy to feint with one of these techniques and to then move into another one.

> *Even if you should decide to specialize in the sporting aspect of BJJ, you should still occasionally grapple wearing shorts and a t-shirt. This will speed up the game and be valuable to you in a self-defence context.*

↗(A) Your opponent is inside your guard.

⇨(B) You use your legs to pull his weight forward a little so that he posts at least one hand on the ground. You come up onto your elbow, and use a hand to grab his wrist.

↘(C) You grab your own wrist to form the figure-four lock. To create the desired leverage against his shoulder, you lie back and scoot your hips around so that you are at a 90-degree angle to him.

↘(D) You secure your opponent's trunk with your legs and rotate his locked arm up towards the ceiling (*see* E), and then toward the floor until he taps.

Triangle choke from the guard

At a beginner's level this technique is usually applied when an opponent tries to pass your guard by putting one arm underneath one of your legs to raise it and then to move around it. To secure the traingle choke it is important to pin his other arm to your chest. As with all submissions, at an intermediate and advanced level, this technique becomes incredibly versatile. It can be set up from working inside the open guard (*see* below) or from the mount, for example.

⇧(A) Your opponent (white) is inside your guard. Using the triangle choke as an attacking technique; first secure your opponent's right arm across your chest.

⇦(B) You then place your right leg in the elbow crease of his left arm.

⬈(C) You then push your opponent's left arm away with your right foot.

⬊(D) This clears the way for you to transition your right calf over the back of his neck at a 90-degree angle.

Once you have practised the illustrated attacks from the guards in isolation, start implementing them in the form of limited sparring. You attack with either the straight armbar, the Kimura, the triangle choke, the frontal choke or the guillotine while your opponent counters. Alternatively, you could execute one of the two basic sweeps. You then change roles as you go into his guard.

⇧(E) Keeping firm control of the arm you have captured, you raise your left leg up in preparation for switching your hips sideways and positioning your right calf across the back of his neck.

⇦(F) You hook the foot of your right leg in behind your left knee and bend your left leg to secure the configuration. His head and one arm are now firmly secured between your thighs.

⬀(G) You squeeze your knees together and pull his head forward and down toward your chest (*see* H).

Frontal cross-lapel choke from the guard

Once you have learnt the correct placement of the hands and the scissoring action of the arms, this becomes a useful technique to have in your repertoire, since it requires no repositioning of your torso and can therefore be applied very quickly.

The final scissoring action of this frontal choke may take some practice but properly executed it can take effect very quickly.

⇧(A) Your opponent is inside your guard.

⇨(B) You insert your one hand deep into his collar, going across your body (your left hand to the left side of his neck). Your thumb is pointing inward across the back of his neck, as deep in as you can get it.

⬊(C) Your other hand goes into the other side of his collar, forearms crossed, until your thumbs nearly meet up.

⇩(D) Let your elbows move outward as you pull him down and forward toward your chest.

As to the hand position behind your opponent's head, some exponents place their palms facing forward, others position the backs of their hands against the skull or they make a fist. As long as the configuration is as tight as possible, this decision is a matter of personal preference.

Rear naked strangle

This is the primary submission used by the Gracies in their challenge matches: the famous '*mata leao*'. A useful sparring drill is to allow your training partner to set himself up in the position in photo B and to start sparring from there. This helps eliminate the beginner's panic when he finds himself rear-mounted.

⇧(A) You have flattened out his body, your 'hooks are in', he is lying on his stomach and you are on his back.

⬉(B) You secure his left arm and ensure that the right side of his neck is exposed to your strangle.

⬈(C) Slide your right arm through and around his neck. Make sure that the inside of your elbow joint is perfectly aligned with his windpipe. Put your right hand onto your left upper bicep or shoulder cap.

⬑(D) Bring your left hand up, going over the back of your right wrist and secure it behind the back of his head. Breathe in deeply so as to expand your chest, bring your shoulders back and your elbows in and together.

Guillotine choke from the guard

The guillotine choke is a very versatile technique. Not only can it be applied from the guard, but also from the 'head snap-down' in the clinch from the side mount and as a defence against some of the more common take downs.

(A) You (blue) have your opponent inside your guard, he is leaning forward with his weight on both hands, leaving his neck unprotected.

(B) Let your feet drop to the floor and come up onto your left elbow (similar to the setup for the Kimura and one of the most basic sweeps).

(C) Wrap your right arm around the back of his neck, scooting your hips out a little so as to create space for it to come through.

(D) Grab the hand of your encircling right arm with your left hand. Your positioning should be such that the bony blade of your forearm is against your opponent's windpipe.

(E) Prepare to recross your legs behind your opponent's back as you drop onto the floor.

(F) Pull up with your left hand as you push away with your thighs and hips; arch your back.

Anklelock from inside the guard

Leglocks are very useful since so few people are familiar with them.
They are not to be found in sport wrestling and are forbidden in judo.
Although they are found in BJJ and in shootfighting, and because sambo
players specialize in them, this means that more than half of the grappling community are ignorant of them.

⇦ (A) You (white) wrap your right arm around his left leg from the outside.

⇗ (B) Secure his ankle tightly, grabbing your own *kimono* for additional support if needed. His left foot is clamped under your right armpit.

⇩ (C) Move in close to him so as to have more control of his leg and of his movement.

⇩ (D) You throw your right leg over his left leg as you throw yourself sideways and back. (You want to lie on your side so that you can arch fully, which is impossible if you just fall back straight onto your back).

⇩ (E) Make sure the leg you throw over is bent, pulled up as much as possible and pressed against his legs. (If your leg is extended and the foot is sticking out, he can secure it and attempt a foot or leglock.)

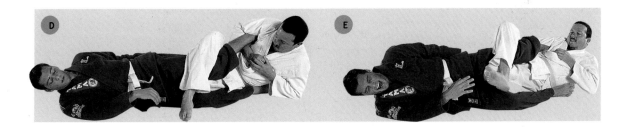

Kneebar from inside the guard

As useful as leglocks may be, they do have one big disadvantage. In executing a leglock you sacrifice control of your opponent's trunk and hips. This means that there is a good chance that a knowledgeable opponent will move as you attempt the technique.

⇦(A) As in the previous technique, you are inside your opponent's guard. Attempt to exert as much control on his body as possible by pushing forward and down against him so as to prevent him moving his hips.

⇨(B) Hook your left arm under his right calf. From this point onward, you must move without hesitation.

⇩(C) Project your right knee over his right thigh as your whole body rotates around his leg.

You can extend the 'guard-sparring game' to include guard passing and leglocks. As you attack from the guard position with your basic sweeps and submissions, your opponent attempts to either pass your guard or apply a basic leglock. This means you are attacking and defending simultaneously.

⇨(D) As in the straight armbar, it is in this transitional phase that you are most at risk of being
countered. Move smoothly but speedily.

⇧(E) Finalize the technique by hugging
his leg to your chest with both hands.
Clamp your knees together as far in as
possible. Push your hips forward and
arch your back to effect the submission.

*When attempting a leglock you
will often find yourself in a
situation in which your opponent tries to counterattack with
a leglock of his own. To get used
to this, both of you can practise
a limited sparring drill that
starts with holding each other's
legs in identical positions. Do
this carefully and slowly as the
knees and ankles are highly
vulnerable to pressure.*

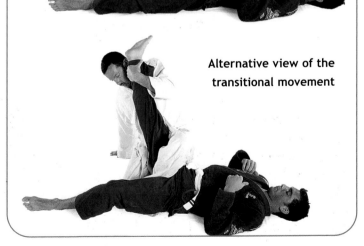

**Alternative view of the
transitional movement**

The concept of joined centres

There are two ways in which you can practise BJJ: either with strength, force and momentum or with sensitivity, relaxation and timing. In the short term the former approach may seem to produce more immediate results but it is only suitable for young athletes, and very little technical growth or learning will take place. A concept taught by the great Rickson Gracie, and one that becomes very evident when one watches footage of him rolling with other BJJ players, is the concept of joined centres. This may not be a concept that beginners are able to implement fully but it is something that they can comprehend and work toward. In this concept, the control and movement principles are integrated with the actions of the opponent, which determine the techniques used.

When your opponent moves, you can resist this movement with a direct opposing force or you can go in the direction he is pushing or pulling you. If you resist him directly then the stronger of the two of you will win. Technique has very little to do with the outcome: when two forces are exerted directly against each other, it is a contest of strength, not one of technique. Instead of opposing force with force, you allow him to lead. As soon as you can feel the direction in which the force is going you can join with it and, you may redirect it, to take you into an advantageous position or technique. To move in union, to roll as one ball made up of two people, you have to join your centre to your opponent's and thus the movement you are executing together has a single centre. If there were two centres, there would be some opposition and strength would then need to be used to overcome it.

This concept of joined centres is a very beautiful and somewhat esoteric concept and one which some of the internal martial arts, like Ba Gua Zhang and Aikido, use extensively. It is nonetheless difficult to bring such a relatively advanced concept to life in a beginner's practice routine.

One of the basic practice drills for developing this type of ability is cooperative rolling; moving from position to position with the eyes closed. By doing so, you are forced to rely on your body's kinaesthetic perception; you cannot strategize or hunt for an opportunity, process this mentally and then attempt to capitalize on it. You feel and respond instantaneously without thinking. There is no winner or loser here, no ego involvement, as none of the positions is held for an extended length of time, the idea being to move continuously. Care has to be taken to keep the movement relaxed and fairly slow. Pay careful attention to your breathing. Initially the tempo will be uneven and your body, and that of your training partner, will come together and drift apart. The idea is to have as few breaks in the movement as possible, and it is especially important that your bodies do not drift apart. Preferably, your arms should stay bent and continuously latched onto your partner's body. Through this you stay close, your bodies stay rounded and, more often than not, the two of you are one rolling ball with one joined centre.

above WIDELY ACCLAIMED AS A GREAT BRAZILIAN JIU JITSU FIGHTER, ROYCE GRACIE, A SECOND GENERATION GRACIE FAMILY MEMBER, KEEPS THIS WIDELY ACCLAIMED MARTIAL ART ALIVE.

Cooperative rolling/joined centres

⇩(A) Your opponent pushes in toward you. Instead of opposing his force with yours, you accommodate yourself to it.

This is only one example to illustrate the concept of cooperative rolling so that your body intuitively understands the concept of joined centres. Try to come up with other examples from your own practice.

⬈(B) As you allow him to push you back, you curl into a ball shape so that you can roll onto your back and hook one of your feet under his thighs.

⇨(C) Maintain muscle tension in your own body only to the degree that is necessary to tip both of you onto your sides, thereby allowing you to further move him with your leg.

⬃(D) Once the momentum starts tipping both of you onto your sides, use the 'hook' you have placed under his thigh to lift his leg and tip him onto his back.

⇩(E) Follow him, thereby ending up mounted on top of him. With good timing, he only becomes aware of the reversal after it has taken place.

Combinations

In most martial arts you would learn single techniques first and then you would move on to learning preset combinations. While it could be said that certain BJJ techniques can often be linked up with each other, it is doubtful whether the practice of rigidly predetermined combinations is very useful.

Whether it is a boxer's jab-cross-hook or a karate practitioner's reverse-punch roundhouse front-kick combination, the differences between the stand-up arts and BJJ are further apparent in the use of combinations. BJJ ground grappling happens at a slower pace than, for instance, an exchange of punches. You can throw a three-punch combination in a fraction of a second and without committing your whole body to the movement. In BJJ, since nearly everything you do is motivated by your core musculature and involves moving your whole body through space, the speed at which two exponents move relative to one another is much slower, for example, than in kickboxing. The idea of throwing a small thunderstorm of techniques at your opponent in the hope that something will penetrate his defences thus cannot exist in BJJ.

It could be said that BJJ is a one-movement-art; you initiate a technique, you read your opponent's reaction, you respond to this, and so forth. This may sound a little simplistic, but it follows naturally from BJJ's emphasis on sensitivity and timing and is a wonderful idea since it takes a lot of the scheming and mind-clutter out of the art. You do not roll and think, you roll and feel and react. At the higher levels of all martial arts you go beyond thinking and move intuitively and responsively, so BJJ simply makes sure that you do this from the beginning. This is also why practising with your eyes closed is so highly recommended (*see* p83). With your eyes open you are strategizing; by the time you react, your opponent has already moved to a different position. With your eyes closed you rely on sensitivity, you do not fall behind and you do not tense up.

Having said this, this does not mean that you cannot develop your own favourite responsive patterns over time. Based on your physical build, psychological preferences, and the fact that certain movement patterns tend to recur or follow each other naturally, it becomes possible to have a game plan of your own. After you have learnt a technique and have understood it sufficiently, you use it in sparring. You observe how your various training partners react to it and then you try to figure out how you can use their reactions to your advantage. After implementing a movement or technique against many sparring partners you will notice that they tend to react in, say, three possible ways. Now you come up with a movement or technique for each of these three reactions. This, in essence, is the creation of combinations and the beginning of your own game plan. It does become apparent that certain techniques work well together, such as alternating a straight armbar with a triangle choke when you are in the guard. This is very different, however, from the usual idea of preset combinations, as they are often taught.

Final considerations on training

In conclusion, some final guidelines on BJJ training might be of use. Remember to move like a river, flowing around obstacles, seeking gaps and establishing control. Always be relaxed and sensitive. You can play a fast and loose ground game or a slow and tight one. You should try the fast-and-loose variation only when you have gone beyond the beginner's level; initially slower and tighter is better.

Each time you go on the mat to 'roll' with your training partner, try working on a problem area. Explore various movement options to see where you are having difficulties. Remember your training partner is there to help you and learn with you, not to be crushed into the mat for the satisfaction of your ego.

Working your movement and escapes is the most important aspect of your training as a beginner. Remember to concentrate on escapes from positions rather than on submission techniques. It is dangerous to focus on trying to escape from an armbar while it is being applied. Rather learn to recognize the set up for the armbar and learn to counter that. The only category of technique that you can try escaping from, as the technique is being applied, is chokes. If in doubt, tap! Be extremely careful of working with neckcranks and heelhooks. These are forbidden in most competitions. Your safety and that of your partner should aways be paramount. Above all else, experiment. If you are practising without joy, you will soon find yourself advertising to sell your second-hand *kimono*. Done in the right spirit, BJJ becomes a highly enjoyable physical chess game. A quote from Machado black belt Chris Haueter comes to mind: 'You want to train as if you are an 80-year-old man who has no strength, no endurance: you relax and let your opponent wear himself out. You become more and more sensitive. Speed, strength and size are all limitations. Knowledge is limitless!'

above PASSING THE GUARD SO AS TO ACHIEVE A SUPERIOR POSITION INVOLVES MOVING OVER, UNDER OR PAST AN OPPONENT'S LEGS.

SELF-DEFENCE

Sport jiu jitsu, especially the Brazilian sport form, has, in recent years, become incredibly popular all over the world. Traditional jiu jitsu is completely combat-oriented with no sporting application, while Brazilian jiu jitsu offers three different areas of practice: sport-tournament play, the set practice of self-defence techniques and Vale Tudo no-holds-barred challenge matches. The sport aspect of BJJ provides a safe and enjoyable way of working one's timing, sensitivity and other important attributes. The self-defence techniques provide retaliatory options in case of a street assault while Vale Tudo fights allow advanced practitioners to pressure-test their abilities. It would be difficult to find a martial-art style more rounded than that and better able to prepare you for any form of street assault.

Street survival

Following is a selection of some of the more important techniques you might want to use should you ever be involved in a street fight. It may also put your martial-arts training into perspective: grim practice based on paranoia or on fantasies of being some kind of super hero is not a good basis for the application of your martial-arts training. However, a commitment to the style and school most suitable for you can become a satisfying and enriching experience that will continue for the rest of your life.

Defence against weapons

When it comes to defending yourself against a weapon wielded by a skilful and determined attacker, your chances are somewhere between slim and none. The so-called experts selling self-defence courses would like you to believe otherwise, and Hollywood makes it appear easy to defend yourself against multiple armed attackers, but police reports and statistics paint a different picture.

It is not impossible to *survive* such a situation, however, but the chances are high that you will be injured in the process. The best defence against weapons is prevention: avoiding at-risk behaviour and locations in the first place, and being aware. Once you find yourself in a potentially dangerous situation, however, the next best option is flight. Carrying a gun is also a great equalizer. As your attacker starts threatening you with his weapon, you point your gun at him. If, however, you do not carry a gun, look around to see if you can find any objects that you could use as an improvised weapon. Chairs, benches and rubbish bins are all very useful to respond physically to such a threat.

If you have no option but to use jiu jitsu to defend yourself, and if a weapon is not being held against you yet, you will need to talk your way into close-combat range of your opponent, grovelling and pleading as you do so. If, however, your attacker has a gun and intends to shoot you and he is a few metres away from you, he will do so nonetheless; no martial art in the world will save you. If, however, he is moving toward you with a knife, slashing and stabbing, and you cannot run, try to get off his line of attack as you move in and attempt to control the hand carrying the knife. Then, maintaining control, counterattack.

If your knife-wielding attacker is at a distance from you, trying to dominate, intimidate and control you with threats, try to close the gap between the two of you. Attempting to grab and control a wrist that is a few centimetres away from your chest is immeasurably easier than trying to grab one that is half a metre away. You need to remember that action beats reaction, and

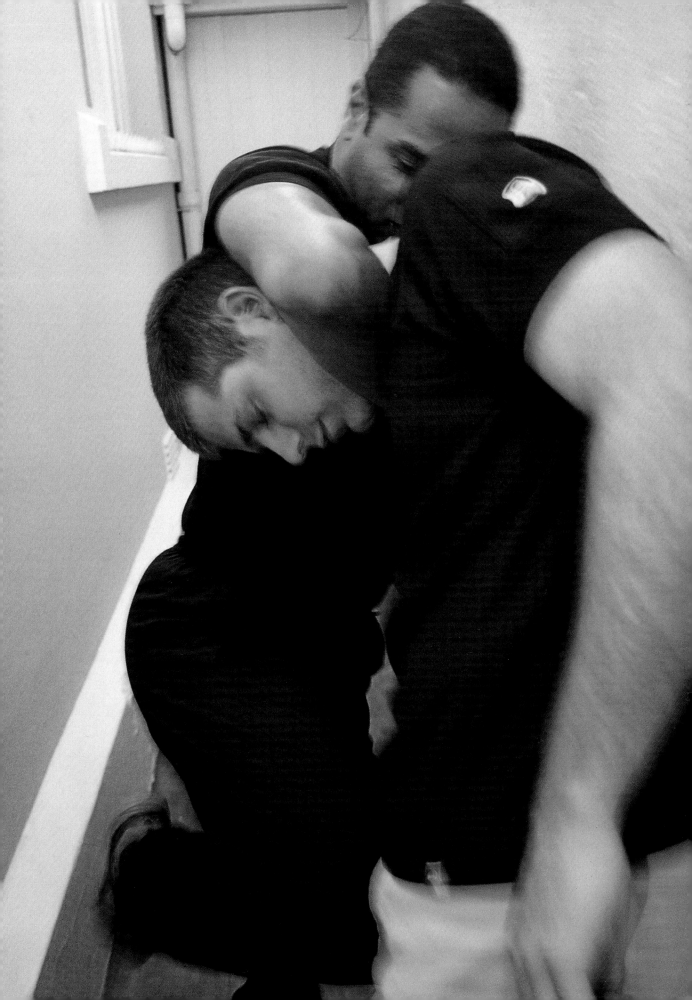

it will take your opponent a few seconds to realize that the person he saw as a sheep has suddenly turned into a wolf. This is known as reflex lag and may be the only thing preventing your sudden demise. Closing a gap of one or two metres between you and your attacker will enable you to respond quickly to his attacks.

Defence against weapons in the days of the *samurai* was different to modern self-defence methods. Then, a jiu jitsu practitioner was seldom unarmed. The reason why classical jiu jitsu includes so many counters to wrist grabs was that, in attacking a *samurai*, a fighter would first grab his wrist to prevent him from unsheathing his sword, then attack him. Technically unarmed defences against a *samurai* sword, or a short sword or dagger, were predicated on the long arcing slashes that were most commonly executed with these weapons. Modern street criminals use their knives in a very different way; in a mad mix of short slashes, stabs and hacking motions, they create a thicket of movement that's very difficult to penetrate. Defences against handguns did not exist in most classical jiu jitsu schools, as handguns (as opposed to rifles) were not a common weapon in medieval times, or in the Tokugawa era in Japan.

Defence against straight attack with baton

↗(A) An attacker is threatening to thrust at your stomach with a baton or a broken bottle.

↗(B) You move off the line of attack.

⇨(C) You secure his wrist and simultaneously execute a strike to his nose, eyes or throat.

⇦(D) Stepping behind him and keeping your hand on his face, you throw him to the ground over your extended leg.

Defence against multiple attackers

Multiple attackers

Another consideration in terms of self-defence is that of multiple attackers. Should you be unarmed when facing multiple armed opponents, and flight is not an option, your chances of survival are minimal. Unless your skill level is phenomenally higher than that of the attackers, or you are armed and they are not, survival against multiple attackers is definitely based on flight. If you can get away without any physical contact, this would be ideal. If the attackers are closing in too fast, you need to break out. If possible, never break out through the centre of a line of men advancing on you; appear as though you are moving into the trap toward the centre, then veer off sharply and crash through either end of it. If you can do so with very little contact, this would be optimal. If you need to make contact, let it be as minimal as possible. Always use strikes, never clinch or grapple. The moment you start clinching or grappling, you are giving the other assailants time to close in on you. Sometimes, in an apparently hopeless situation, it may be feasible to pick out the leader and drive into him with a strong barrage of multiple strikes. This may cause the others to have second thoughts of attacking you. Then again it may make them all the more determined to hospitalize you.

Admittedly, there are those who have survived attacks by more than one person. If you are a trained jiu jitsu practitioner in a potentially dangerous situation, you will defend yourself as best you can. If you have been trained well your chances of survival will be good.

(A) Two attackers have managed to execute a surprise attack and have secured your arms.

(B) Slightly unbalance one of the attackers with your arm and set up your body for a low kick. Alternatively, once you have freed one of your hands, it may be preferable to execute a hand attack to a vital area such as the throat or the groin.

(C) If possible, attempt to execute a low side thrust kick to his knee.

(D) This frees you and allows you to turn and side kick the second attacker in the knee.

Situational factors

Combat never happens in a vacuum, so use your environment to your full advantage. Awareness being of primary concern, immediately look for all possible escape routes and use the best one if there is still time. If you cannot escape, look for any improvised weapons such as a rock, a piece of brick, a broken bottle or a stick. If it can be thrown, throw it. If you can hit your opponent with it, do so. If you are at the beach, scoop up a handful of sand and throw it into your attacker's eyes. If it's daytime and you are outside make sure that the sun is behind you and shining into his eyes.

Your friend the wall

As regards using the environment, mention should be made of walls. A wall is a wonderful thing. When you face multiple attackers it keeps your back covered. It

above FIGHTS ARE OFTEN NOT WON BY THE MOST SKILLED FIGHTER BUT BY THE PERSON WHO IS PREPARED TO ESCALATE THE LEVEL AND INTENSITY OF VIOLENCE MORE QUICKLY THAN HIS OPPONENT, IN THIS INSTANCE BY USING A RUBBISH BIN AS AN IMPROVISED WEAPON.

is also most useful for running people into. If you knock someone's head into it, the fight is usually over. Pushing someone against a wall limits their mobility and allows you to control them, to set up strikes or take downs. You can accelerate yourself off the wall, be it for a quicker getaway or greater impact for an attack. If it is not too high you can pull yourself up and over it so as to escape. It is amazingly versatile and, unless you are fighting on a soccer field or a beach, there's always one close by and just waiting to be used.

Him up, you down

One of the more unpleasant situations in which you can find yourself is where you are sitting or lying on the ground, with your attacker standing over you, kicking and stomping you.

With some training, this situation becomes far less threatening than it at first appears. Brazilian jiu jitsu may well have the best answer to this problem.

The first of the two techniques consists of you lying on your back, the soles of your feet pointing at your attacker. Should you land on the floor in any position other than this, move into this position as quickly as possible. His kicks can no longer reach your head and torso, and every time he attempts to kick you, you kick back at him or block his kicks by ramming your shoe into his shin. If he tries to circle you, use the rocking motion of your trunk, and with the assistance of your arms, turn yourself, track his movement and maintain your position in relation to him. This is easy and quite enjoyable to practise in a classroom setting as long as both parties are barefoot.

The second technique to use under these circumstances ensures that you get up safely without being kicked or punched in the head. You support your weight on one hand and the opposite foot. Your other hand protects your face as you rock forward and kick with the free leg. You then rock backward, raise your hips as much as possible, bringing the kicking leg through underneath your body and scooting back as far as far as you can to stand up into a fighting position. In doing so, create enough distance as your opponent may be moving toward you.

above A WELL-PLACED KNEESTRIKE TO THE GROIN, AS ILLUSTRATED, CAN LEAVE YOUR OPPONENT WEAK ON HIS FEET.

A few final thoughts

- Don't be a hero. It is not a matter of winning all your fights but a matter of never losing one. A fight avoided is a fight you have not lost.

- Always keep it simple. A strike to the throat is better than a wrist-locking sequence that consists of five separate movements.

- In training to defend yourself, ensure the specific techniques you are learning are commonly used in street attacks. Rear-hand swinging haymaker punches, rugby tackles and close-range head butts are common attacks, head-high roundhouse kicks and attacks with *samurai* swords are not.

- Don't allow anyone into extreme close range, if possible. Keep a safe distance to any potential threat.

- Learn to breakfall properly. It is as useful a skill to use in self-defence as in falling down a staircase or off a motorbike.

- Learn a few basic techniques well rather than many techniques badly.

- Ensure that a large part of your training is done in an alive manner against a resisting opponent with plenty of movement, energy and impact.

- Do some training outdoors, in the kind of environment and weather conditions in which you might find yourself if you are assaulted.

- Keep yourself in decent physical shape. If you are out of breath after sprinting 50m, your fight-or-flight option disappears and you are forced to fight. If the fight lasts longer than 10 or 20 seconds, running out of gas can be extremely hazardous.

- Always be aware of your environment and the people in it. Do not assume that bad things cannot happen to good people. If you are caught by surprise, it may all be over very quickly. In the *dojo* there is an agreement to fight, there are rules and you are training with a partner. An assault, however, is not based on any agreement; there are no rules and you are reacting to an attacker.

- If you wish to know more about real combat, talk to those who have experienced it. Police officers, bouncers, bodyguards and army combat veterans may have much wisdom to impart. In contrast, many highly ranked classical martial arts teachers have never been in a real fight in their lives, nor do they practise their skills in an alive manner. This does not stop them from marketing themselves as self-defence experts. Do not mistake packaging for substance.

- Stay away from the kind of places, people and situations which are likely to mean trouble. Dark alleys at night, single intoxicated men on the prowl in nightclubs and windows or doors carelessly left open are examples of the kind of things you might want to avoid.

- Know the law as it pertains to self-defence. Keeping this in mind, defend yourself until your attacker is no longer capable of continuing with his assault.

GLOSSARY

PORTUGUESE GLOSSARY

Americana:	Figure-four armlock
Baiana:	Double-leg takedown
Cem kilos:	(100 kilos) Side-control position, side mount
Cervical:	Neck crank
Chave de braço:	Armlock
Chave de calcanhar:	Heelhook
Chave de joelho:	Knee-bar leglock
Chave de pe:	Toehold/footlock
Chave de tornozelo:	Anklelock
Chute:	Kick
Cinturada:	Takedown with arms around waist
Cruzifixio:	Crucifix neck-crank
Dar um rola:	To spar or roll with
É katagatami:	Arm-triangle choke
Estrangulomento:	Choke
Faixa azul:	Blue belt, awarded after white belt
Faixa branca:	White belt, first belt worn
Faixa marron:	Brown belt, awarded after purple belt
Faixa preta:	Black belt, awarded after brown belt
Faixa roxa:	Purple belt, awarded after blue belt
Fechas a guarda:	Closing the guard position
Grau:	Dan level, level of black-belt rank
Gravata technica:	Headlock
Guarda aberta:	Open-guard position
Guarda fechada:	Closed-guard position
Guilotinha:	Guillotine choke
Hezekiel:	Forearm choke
Joelho na barriga:	Knee-on-belly position
Joga por baixo:	Play from bottom
Joga por cima:	Play from top
Kimono:	Jiu Jitsu suit, gi
Kimura:	Shoulderlock
Mata leâo:	Killing the lion, rear naked choke
Meia guarda:	Half-guard position
Montada:	Mount position
Muito obrigado/a:	Thank you very much
Passa a guarda:	Passing the guard
Passador:	Someone who passes the guard well
Pedelada:	Heel-stomp kick launched from ground
Pisâo:	Stepping stomp kick, often aimed at knee
Postura:	Posture
Regra:	Rules
Relógio:	Clock choke
Saída:	Exit, escape from inferior position
Saída de quadril:	Hip escape
Tatame:	Mat
Tempo:	Command to stop sparring; time
Triangulo:	Triangle-choke using the legs
Vai:	Command to start sparring; go
Vira a quatro:	Going to the turtle position; on all fours

JAPANESE TERMS

Ashi barai:	Foot sweep
Ashi garami:	Heelhook footlock
Ashi gatame:	Anklelock
Atemi waza:	Striking techniques
Dan:	Black-belt rank
Do basami:	Open-guard position
Do jime:	Closed-guard position
Gatame waza:	Controlling techniques
Gi:	Jiu Jitsu uniform
Hadaka jime:	Rear naked choke
Hakama:	Traditional pants skirt
Heiho:	Study of strategy
Hiji ate waza:	Elbow-striking techniques
Hiza juji gatame:	Knee-bar leglock
Jigoku jime:	Crucifix neck-crank
Jiu:	Soft, gentle (also ju)
Jitsu:	Technique (also jutsu)
Juji gatame:	Straight armbar

GLOSSARY

Jumbi undo:	Warm-up exercises	**Osae komi waza:**	Hold-down techniques
Kami shiho gatame:	Sixty-nine position	**Randori:**	Light free-sparring practice
Kansetsu waza:	Holds and locks	**Rei:**	Bowing
Kata:	Pre-arranged sequence of techniques	**Ryu/ryu-ha:**	School, style
		Sabaki:	Body movement
Kata gatame:	Arm-triangle choke	**Samurai:**	Member of the warrior caste
Kesa gatame:	Scarf-hold position	**Sangaku jime:**	Triangle-choke using the legs
Ki:	Vital energy, internal power	**Shime waza:**	Strangulation techniques
Kime waza:	Shock techniques	**Sutemi waza:**	Sacrifice throws
Kokyu:	Breathing practice, energy gathering	**Tachi waza:**	Standing throwing techniques
		Tate shiho gatame:	Mount position
Kyusho:	Nerve points	**Tori:**	Attacker, person initiating the technique
Maai:	Distance and timing between opponents		
		Ude garami:	Bent armlock
Mae hadaka jime:	Front naked choke, guillotine choke	**Uke:**	Defender, person receiving the technique
Nage waza:	Throwing techniques	**Ukemi waza:**	Breakfalling technique
Ne waza:	Ground grappling techniques	**Ushiro tate shiho gatame:**	Rear-mounted position

MAKING CONTACT

While Brazilian Jiu Jitsu ranking standards and lineage are verified by means of the international organisation in Brazil, such criteria may vary in the classical and hybrid styles. There are many good styles and clubs out there. These are merely a selection.

INTERNATIONAL CLASSICAL & HYBRID JIU JITSU ASSOCIATIONS

AMERICA
■ **AMERICAN JUDO & JU JITSU FEDERATION**
c/o Central Office Administrator
P.O. Box 7018, Chico, CA 95927
■ E-mail: co@ajjf.org
■ Website:
www.ajjf.org/ajjf.html

■ **PETCO COMMUNITY SERVICE ROOM**
■ Petco, 26501 Bouquet, Canyon Rd, Sanyas, CA 91 3500
■ Website: www.budoshin.com

AUSTRALIA
■ **AUSTRALIA JU JITSU FEDERATION**
■ 8 Tahoe Place, Robina, Queensland, 4226
■ Tel: (+7) 5562 0630
■ Website: www.jujitsu.com.au

BRITAIN
■ **BRITISH JU-JITSU ASSOCIATION**
■ 5 Avenue Parade, Accrington, Lancashire, BB5 6PN
■ Website: www.bjjagb.com

GERMANY
■ **DEUTSCHER JU JITSU VERBAND e.V.**
■ Paul Rohland Street 2, 06712 Zeitz
■ Website:
www.ju-jutsu-net.de

SOUTH AFRICA
■ **VALE TUDO JIU JITSU**
■ 6 Surrey Road, Mowbray, 7700 Cape Town
■ Website:
www.valetudojiujitsu.com

INTERNATIONAL BRAZILIAN JIU JITSU ASSOCIATIONS

AUSTRALIA
■ **BRAZILIAN JIU JITSU AUSTRALIA**
■ John Will's Brazilian Jiu Jitsu Academy, 159A Malop Street, Geelong, Victoria
■ Tel: (+3) 5244 3084
■ Website: www.bjj.com.au

BRAZIL
■ **INTERNATIONAL BRAZILIAN JIU JITSU FEDERATION**
■ Avenida Comandante Júlio de Moura 276, 22620–010, Barra da Tijuca, Rio de Janeiro
■ Tel: (+21) 2493 4929
■ Fax: (+21) 2491 6901

CANADA
■ **MARCUS SOARES BRAZILIAN JIU JITSU**
■ 751 Burley Place, West Vancouver, British Columbia, VJT 2AZ
■ Tel: (+604) 922 4865
■ Website:
http://bjjholland.gamepoint.net

FRANCE
■ **ECOLE D'ARTS MARTIAUX BRASILIENS**
■ Cote d'Azur, Cannes, Dojo Ranguin, Avenue de la Borde, La Bocca, Cannes
■ Tel: (+6) 2282 1618

HOLLAND
■ **BRAZILIAN JIU JITSU HOLLAND**
■ Budovereniging Asahi, 83 St Crispijnstraat, Waalwijk

UK
■ **BRAZILIAN TOP TEAM**
■ Queen Mother Sports Centre, 223 Vauxhall Bridge Road, London GB, SW1V 1EL

SOUTH AFRICA
■ **NOVAGEN ACADEMY**
■ Game City, Stamford Hill Road, Stamford Hill, 4001, Durban
■ Website: www.geocities.com/novagen_jiujitsu

INDEX

PHOTOGRAPHIC CREDITS

All photography by Nick Aldrige, with the exception of those supplied by the following photographers and/or agencies (copyright rests with these individuals and/or their agencies):

4	Christopher Domitter	18	David Roberts
5	Christopher Domitter	19	David Roberts
8	David Roberts	22	David Roberts
8	Christopher Domitter	28	David Roberts
10	Bridgeman Art Library/The Stapleton Collection	42	David Roberts
		46	Ryno Reyneke
13	Hurd Evan/Corbis Sygma	47	David Roberts
14	David Roberts	82	Hurd Evan/Corbis Sygma
15	David Roberts		